William Taylor Adams

Breaking away

The fortunes of a student

William Taylor Adams

Breaking away
The fortunes of a student

ISBN/EAN: 9783337269043

Printed in Europe, USA, Canada, Australia, Japan

Cover: Foto ©Andreas Hilbeck / pixelio.de

More available books at **www.hansebooks.com**

THE REBELLION IN THE FAIRVILLE LIBERAL INSTITUTE. — Page 38.

Oliver Optic's

Starry Flag Series

BREAKING AWAY

Lee & Shepard

BOSTON

BREAKING AWAY;

OR,

THE FORTUNES OF A STUDENT.

BY

OLIVER OPTIC,

AUTHOR OF "YOUNG AMERICA ABROAD," "THE ARMY AND NAVY STORIES,"
"THE WOODVILLE STORIES," "THE BOAT-CLUB STORIES,"
"THE RIVERDALE STORIES," ETC.

———————

BOSTON:
LEE AND SHEPARD.
1868.

ELECTROTYPED AT THE

BOSTON STEREOTYPE FOUNDRY,

No. 19 Spring Lane.

TO

My Young Friend,

HARLAN P. BALLARD,

𝔗𝔥𝔦𝔰 𝔅𝔬𝔬𝔨

IS AFFECTIONATELY DEDICATED.

THE STARRY FLAG SERIES,

BY OLIVER OPTIC.

TO BE COMPLETED IN SIX VOLUMES.

I. THE STARRY FLAG; or, The Young Fisherman of
Cape Ann.

II. BREAKING AWAY; or, The Fortunes of a Student.

III. SEEK AND FIND; or, The Adventures of a Smart
Boy.

Others in preparation.

(4)

PREFACE.

"BREAKING AWAY" is the second of the series of stories published in "OUR BOYS AND GIRLS," and the author had no reason to complain of the reception accorded to it by his young friends, as it appeared in the weekly issues of the Magazine; but, on the contrary, he finds renewed occasion cordially to thank them for their continued appreciation of his earnest efforts to please them.

After an experience of more than twenty years as a teacher, the writer did not expect his young friends to sympathize with the schoolmaster of this story, for doubtless many of them have known and despised a similar creature in real life. Mr. Parasyte is not a myth; but we are grateful that an enlightened public sentiment is every year rendering more and more odious the petty tyrant of the school-room, and we are too happy to give this retreating personage a parting blow as he retires from the scene of his fading glories.

Rebellions, either in the school or in the state, are always dangerous and demoralizing; but while we unequivocally condemn the tyrant in our story, we cannot always approve the conduct of his pupils. One evil gives birth to another; but even a righteous end cannot justify immoral means, and we beg to remind our young and enthusiastic readers that Ernest Thornton and his friends were compelled to acknowledge that they had done wrong in many things, and that "Breaking Away" was deemed a very doubtful expedient for the redress even of a real wrong.

As it was impossible for Ernest to relate the whole of his eventful history in one volume, Breaking Away will be immediately followed by a sequel, — "Seek and Find," — in which the hero will narrate his adventures in seeking and finding his mother, of whose tender care he was deprived from his earliest childhood.

HARRISON SQUARE, MASS.,
September 23, 1867.

CONTENTS.

CHAPTER VIII.

CHAPTER IX.

CHAPTER X.

CHAPTER XI.

CHAPTER XII.

CHAPTER XIII.

CHAPTER XIV.

CHAPTER XV.

CHAPTER XVI.

CHAPTER XVII.

CHAPTER XVIII.

CHAPTER XIX.

CHAPTER XX.

CHAPTER XXI.

CHAPTER XXII.

CHAPTER XXIII.

CHAPTER XXIV.

CHAPTER XXV.

CHAPTER XXVI.

BREAKING AWAY;

OR,

THE FORTUNES OF A STUDENT.

CHAPTER I.

IN WHICH ERNEST THORNTON INTRODUCES HIMSELF.

ERNEST THORNTON!" called Mr. Parasyte, the principal of the Parkville Liberal Institute, in a tone so stern and severe that it was impossible to mistake his meaning, or not to understand that a tempest was brewing. "Ernest Thornton!"

As that was my name, I replied to the summons by rising, and exhibiting my full length to all the boys assembled in the school-room — about one hundred in number.

"Ernest Thornton!" repeated Mr. Parasyte, not satisfied with the demonstration I had made.

"Sir!" I replied, in a round, full, square tone, which was intended to convince the principal that I was ready to "face the music."

"Ernest Thornton, I am informed that you have been engaged in a fight," he continued, in a tone a little less sharp than that with which he had pronounced my name; and I had the vanity to believe that the square tone in which I had uttered the single word I had been called upon to speak had produced a salutary impression upon him.

"I haven't been engaged in any fight, sir," I replied, with all the dignity becoming a boy of fourteen.

"Sir! what do you mean by denying it?" added Mr. Parasyte, working himself up into a magnificent mood, which was intended to crush me by its very majesty — but it didn't.

"I have not engaged in any fight, sir," I repeated, with as much decision as the case seemed to require.

"Didn't you strike William Poodles?" demanded he, fiercely.

"Yes, sir, I did. Bill Poodles hit me in the head,

and I knocked him over in self-defence — that was all, sir."

"Don't you call that a fight, sir?" said Mr. Parasyte, knitting his brows, and looking savage enough to swallow me.

"No, sir; I do not. I couldn't stand still and let him pound me."

"You irritated him in the beginning, and provoked him to strike the blow. I hold you responsible for the fight."

"I had no intention to irritate him, and I did not wish to provoke him."

"I hold you responsible for the fight, Thornton," said the principal again.

I supposed he would, for Poodles was the son of a very wealthy and aristocratic merchant in the city of New York, while I belonged to what the principal regarded as an inferior order of society. At least twenty boys in the Parkville Liberal Institute came· upon the recommendation of Poodle's father, while not a single one had been lured into these classic shades by the influence of my family — if I could be said to belong to any family.

2

Besides, I was but a day scholar, and my uncle paid only tuition bills for me, while most of the pupils were boarders at the Institute.

I am writing of events which took place years ago, but I have seen no reason to change the opinion then formed, that Mr. Parasyte, the principal, was a "toady" of the first water; that he was a narrow-minded, partial man, in whom the principle of justice had never been developed. He was a good teacher, an excellent teacher; by which I mean only to say that he had a rare skill and tact for imparting knowledge, the mere dry bones of art, science, and philosophy. He was a capital scholar himself, and a capital teacher; but that is the most that can be said of him.

I have no hesitation in saying that his influence upon the boys was bad, as that of every narrow-minded, partial, and unjust man must be; and if I had any boys to send away to a boarding school, they should go to a good and true man, even if I knew him to be, intellectually, an inferior teacher, rather than to such a person as Mr. Parasyte. He "toadied" to the rich boys, and oppressed the poorer ones. Poodles was the most important boy in the school, and he was never punished for his faults, which were not few, nor compelled to learn his lessons, as other boys were. But I think Poodles hated the magnate of the Parkville Liberal Institute as much as any other boy.

Parkville is situated on Lake Adieno, a beautiful sheet of water, twenty miles in length, in the very heart of the State of New York. The town was a thriving place of four thousand inhabitants, at which a steamboat stopped twice every day in her trip around the lake. The academy was located at the western verge of the town, while my home was about a mile beyond the eastern line of the village.

I lived with my uncle, Amos Thornton. His residence was a vine-clad cottage, built in the Swiss style, on the border of the lake, the lawn in front of it extending down to the water's edge. My uncle was a strange man. He had erected this cottage ten years before the time at which my story opens, when I was a mere child. He had employed in the beginning, before the house was completed, a man and his wife as gardener and housekeeper, and they had been residents in the cottage ever since.

I said that my uncle was a strange man; and so he was. He hardly ever spoke a word to any one, and never unless it was absolutely necessary to do so. He was not one of the talking kind; and old Jerry, the gardener, and old Betsey, the house-keeper, seemed to have been cast in the same mould. I never heard them talking to each other, and they certainly never spoke to me unless I asked them a question, and then only in the briefest manner.

I never knew what to make of my uncle Amos. He had a little room, which he called his library, in one corner of the house, which could be entered only by passing through his bedroom. In this apart-ment he spent most of his time, though he went out to walk every day, while I was at school; but, if he saw me coming, he always retreated to the house. He was gloomy and misanthropic; he never went to church himself, though he always compelled me to go, and also to attend the Sunday school. He did not go into society, and had little or noth-

ing to do with, or to say to, the people of Parkville. He never troubled them, and they were content to let him alone.

As may well be supposed, my life at the cottage
was not the pleasantest that could be imagined.
It was hardly a home, only a stopping-place to
me. It was gloom and silence there, and my uncle was the lord of the silent land. Such a life was
not to my taste, and I envied the boys and girls
of my acquaintance in Parkville, as I saw them
talking and laughing with their fathers and moth-
ers, their brothers and sisters, or gathered in the
social circle around the winter fire. It seemed to
me that their cup of joy was full, while mine was
empty. I longed for friends and companions to
share with me the cares and the pleasures of life.

Of myself I knew little or nothing. My memory
hardly reached farther back than the advent of my
uncle at Lake Adieno, and all my early associations
were connected with the cottage and its surroundings. I had a glimmering and indistinct idea of
something before our coming to Parkville. It seemed
to me that I had once known a motherly lady

2*

with a sweet and lovely expression on her face; and I had a faint recollection of looking out upon a dreary waste of waters; but I could not fix the idea distinctly in my mind. I supposed that the lady was my mother. I made several vain efforts to induce my uncle to tell me something about her; if he knew anything, he would not tell me.

Old Jerry and his wife evidently had no knowledge whatever in regard to me before my uncle brought me to Parkville. They could not tell me anything, and my uncle would not. Though I was a boy of only fourteen, this concealment of my birth and parentage troubled me. I was told that my father was dead; and this was all the information I could obtain. Where he had lived, when and where he died, I was not permitted to know. If I asked a question, my uncle turned on his heel and left me, with no reply.

The vision of the motherly lady, distant and indistinct as it was, haunted me like a familiar melody. If the person was my mother, why should her very name be kept from me? If she was still living, why could I not go to her? If she was dead, why might I not water the green sod above her grave with my tears, and plant the sweetest flowers by her tombstone? I was dissatisfied with my lot, and I was determined, at no distant day, to wring from my silent uncle the particulars of my early history. I was so eager to get this knowledge that I was almost ready to take him by the throat, if need be, and force out the truth from between his closed lips.

I never had an opportunity to speak with him; but I could make the opportunity. He took no notice of me; he avoided me; he seemed hardly to be conscious of my existence. Yet he was not a hard man, in the common sense of the word. He clothed me as well as the best boys in the Institute. If I wanted anything for the table, old Jerry was ordered to procure it. When I was ten years old a little row-boat was furnished for me; but before I was fourteen I wanted something better, and told my uncle so. He made me no reply; but on my next birthday a splendid sail-boat floated on the lake before the house, which Jerry said had been built for me. I told my silent lord that I was much obliged to him for his very acceptable present, when I happened to catch him on the lawn. He turned on his heel, and fled as though I had stung him with the sting of ingratitude.

If I wanted anything, I had only to mention it; and no one criticised my conduct, whatever I did. I was free to go and come when I pleased; and though in vacation I was absent three days at once in my boat, no one asked me where I had been, or what I had done. Neither my uncle nor his silent satellites ever expressed a fear that I might be drowned in my voyages in night and storm on the lake; and I came to the conclusion that no one would care if I were lost.

I do not know how, under such a home government, I ever became a decent fellow. I do not know why I am not now a pirate, a freebooter, a pickpocket, or a nuisance to myself and the world in some other capacity. I have come to believe since that my inherited good qualities saved me under such an utter neglect of all home influences. It is a marvel to me that I was not ruined before I was twenty-one; and from the deepest depths of my heart I thank God for his mercy in sparing me from the fate which generally and naturally overtakes such a neglected child.

At the age of twelve, after I had passed through the common school of the town, I was admitted to the Parkville Liberal Institute, which I wished to attend because a friend of mine in the town was there. My uncle did not object — he never objected to anything. Without pride or vanity I may say that I was a good scholar, and I took the highest rank at the academy. When I was about twelve years old, some instructions which I received in the Sunday school produced a strong impression on my mind, and led me to take my stand for life. I tried to be true to God and myself, to be just and manly in all things. Whatever the world may sneeringly say of goodness and truth, I am sure that I owe my popularity among the boys of the Parkville Liberal Institute to these endeavors — not always successful — to do right.

CHAPTER II.

IN WHICH THERE IS TROUBLE IN THE PARKVILLE
LIBERAL INSTITUTE.

I WISH to say in the beginning, and once for all, that I did not set myself up as a saint, or even as a model boy. I made no pretensions, but I did try to be good and true. I felt that I had no one in this world to rely upon for my future; everything depended upon myself alone, and I realized the responsibility of building up my own character. I do not mean to assert that I had all these ideas and purposes clearly defined in my own mind; only that I had a simple abstract desire to be good, and to do good, without knowing precisely in what the being and the doing consisted. My notions, many of them, I am now aware, were crude and undefined.

I have observed that I was a favorite among the

boys of the Institute, a kind of leader and oracle among them, though I was not fully conscious of the fact at the time. While I now think I owe the greater portion of the esteem and regard in which I was held by my companions to my desire to be good and true, I must acknowledge that other circumstances had their influence upon them. I was the owner of the best boat on Lake Adieno, and to the boys this was a matter of no small consequence. There were half a dozen row-boats belonging to the academy, but nothing that carried a sail.

I always had money. I had only to ask my uncle for any sum I wanted, and it was given me, without a question as to its intended use. I mention the fact to his discredit, and it would have been a luxury to me to have had him manifest interest enough in my welfare to refuse my request.

I was naturally enterprising and fearless, and was therefore foremost in all feats of daring, in all trials of skill in athletic games. Indeed, to sum up the estimate which was made of me by my associates in

school and the people of Parkville, I was "a smart
boy." Perhaps my vanity was tickled once or twice
by hearing this appellation applied to me; but I am
sure I was not spoiled by the favor with which I
was regarded.

Though I was not an unhappy boy, there was an
aching void in my heart which I could not fill, a
longing for such a home as hundreds of my young
friends enjoyed; and I would gladly have exchanged
the freedom from restraint for which others envied
me for the poorest home in the town, where I could
have been welcomed by a fond mother, where I
could have had a kind father to feel an interest
in me.

During the spring, summer, and autumn months,
when the wind and weather would permit, I went
to school in my sail-boat. My course lay along the
shore, and if I was becalmed and likely to be tardy,
I had only to moor my craft, and take to the road.
At the noon intermission, therefore, my boat was
available for use, and I always had a party.

On the day that I was called up charged with
fighting, the Splash — for that was the suggestive

name I had chosen for my trim little craft — was lying at the boat pier on the lake in front of the Institute building. The forenoon session of the school had just closed, and I had gone to the boat to eat my dinner, which I always carried in the stern locker.

Before I had finished, Bill Poodles came down with an Arithmetic in his hand. It was the dinner hour of the boarding students, and I wondered that Bill was not in the refectory. Our class had a difficult lesson in arithmetic that day, which I had worked out in the solitude of my chamber at the cottage the preceding evening. The students had been prohibited, under the most severe penalty, from assisting each other; and it appeared that Bill had vainly applied to half a dozen of his classmates for help: none of them dared to afford it.

Bill Poodles was a disagreeable fellow, arrogant and "airy" as he was lazy and stupid. I doubt whether he ever learned a difficult task alone. The arithmetic lesson was a review of the principles which the class had gone over, and consisted of a dozen examples, printed on a slip of paper, to test the knowl-

3

edge of the students; and it was intimated that those who failed would be sent down into a lower class. Bill dreaded anything like a degradation. He was proud, if he was lazy. He knew that I had performed the examples, and while his fellow-boarders were at dinner, he had stolen the opportunity to appeal to me for the assistance he so much needed.

Though Bill was a disagreeable fellow, and though, in common with a majority of the students, I disliked him, I would willingly have assisted him if the prohibition to do so had not been so emphatic. Mr. Parasyte was so particular in the present instance, that the following declaration had been printed on the examination paper, and each boy was required to sign it: —

"*I declare upon my honor, that I have had no assistance whatever in solving these examples, and that I have given none to others.*"

Bill begged me to assist him. I reasoned with him, and told him he had better fail in the review than forfeit his honor by subscribing to a falsehood. He made light of my scruples; and then I told him

I had already signed my own paper, and would not falsify my statement.

"Humph!" exclaimed he, with a sneer. "You hadn't given any one assistance when you signed, but you can do it now, and it will be no lie."

I was indignant at the proposition, it was so mean and base; and I expressed myself squarely in regard to it. I had finished my dinner, and, closing the locker, stepped out of the boat upon the pier. Bill followed me, begging and pleading till I was disgusted with him. I told him then that I would not do what he asked if he teased me for a month. He was angry, and used insulting language. I turned on my heel to leave him. He interpreted this movement on my part as an act of cowardice, and, coming up behind me, struck me a heavy blow on the back of the head with his fist. He was on the point of following it up with another, when, though he was eighteen years old, and half a foot taller than I was, I hit him fairly in the eye, and knocked him over backwards, off the pier, and into the lake.

A madder fellow than Bill Poodles never floundered in shallow water. The lake where he fell was not more than two or three feet deep, and doubtless its soft bosom saved him from severe injury. He picked himself up, and, dripping from his bath, rushed to the shore. He was insane with passion. Seizing a large stone, he hurled it at me. I moved towards him, with the intention of checking his demonstration, when his valor was swallowed up in discretion, and he rushed towards the school building.

For this offence I was brought to the bar of Mr. Parasyte's uneven justice. Poodles had told his own story after changing his drabbled garments. It was unfortunate that there were no witnesses of the affray, for the principal would sooner have doubted the evidence of his own senses than the word of Bill Poodles, simply because it was not politic for him to do so. My accuser declared that he had spoken civilly and properly to me, and that I had insulted him. He had walked up to me, and placed his hand upon my shoulder, simply to attract my attention, when I had struck him a severe blow in the face, which had knocked him over backwards into the lake.

In answer to this charge, I told the truth exactly as it was. Bill acknowledged that he had asked me some questions about the review lesson, which I had declined to answer. He was sorry he had offended so far, but was not angry at my refusal. He had determined to sacrifice his dinner, and his play during the intermission, to enable him to perform the examples. I persisted in the statement I had already made, and refused to modify it in any manner. It was the simple truth.

"Ernest Thornton," said Mr. Parasyte, solemnly, "hitherto I have regarded you with favor. I have looked upon you as a worthy and deserving boy; and I confess my surprise and grief at the event of to-day. Not content with the dastardly assault committed upon William Poodles, — whose devotion to his duty and his studies has been manifested by the sacrifice of his dinner, — you utter the most barefaced falsehood which it was ever my misfortune to hear a boy tell."

"I have told the truth, sir!" I exclaimed, my cheek burning with indignation.

"Silence, sir! Such conduct and such a boy

3 *

cannot be tolerated at the Parkville Liberal Institute. But in consideration of your former good conduct, I purpose to give you an opportunity to redeem your character."

"My character don't need any redeeming," I declared, stoutly.

"I see you are in a very unhappy frame of mind, and I fear you are incorrigible. But I must do my duty, and I proceed to pronounce your sentence, which is, that you be expelled from the Parkville Liberal Institute."

"Bill Poodles is the biggest liar in the school!" shouted a daring little fellow among my friends, who were astounded at the result of the examination, and at the sentence.

"That's so!" said another.

"Yes!" "Yes!" "Yes!" shouted a dozen more. "Throw him over! Bill Poodles is the liar!"

Mr. Parasyte was appalled at this demonstration — a demonstration which never could have occurred without the provocation of the grossest injustice. The boys were well disciplined, and the order of the Institute was generally unexceptionable. Such a flurry had never before been known, and it was evident that the students intended to take the law into their own hands. They acted upon the impulse of the moment, and I judged that at least one half of them were engaged in the demonstration.

Poodles was a boy of no principle; he was notorious as a liar; and the boys regarded it as an outrage upon themselves and upon me that he should be believed, while my story appeared to have no weight whatever.

Mr. Parasyte trembled, not alone with rage, but with fear. The startling event then transpiring threatened the peace, if not the very existence, of the Parkville Liberal Institute. I folded my arms, — for I felt my dignity, — and endeavored to be calm, though my bosom heaved and bounded with emotion.

"Boys — young gentlemen, I — " the principal began.

"Throw him over! Put him out!" yelled the students, excited beyond measure.

"Young gentlemen!" shouted Mr. Parasyte.

"Three cheers for Ernest Thornton!" hoarsely screamed Bob Hale, my intimate friend and long-time "crony."

They were given with an enthusiasm which bordered on infatuation.

"Will you hear me, students?" cried Mr. Parasyte.

"No!" "No!" "No!"   "Throw him over!" "Put him out!"

The scene was almost as unpleasant to me as to the principal, proud as I was of the devotion of my friends. I did not wish to be vindicated in such a way, and I was anxious to put a stop to such disorderly proceedings. I raised my hand in an appealing gesture.

"Fellow-students," said I; and the school-room was quiet.

CHAPTER III.

IN WHICH ERNEST IS EXPELLED FROM THE PARK-VILLE LIBERAL INSTITUTE.

FELLOW-STUDENTS," I continued, when the school-room was still enough for me to be heard, "I am willing to submit to the rules of the Institute, and even to the injustice of the principal. For my sake, as well as for your own, behave like men."

I folded my arms, and was silent again. I felt that it was better to suffer than to resist, and such an exhibition of rowdyism was not to my taste. I glanced at Mr. Parasyte, to intimate to him that he could say what he pleased; and he took the hint.

"Young gentlemen, this is a new experience to me. In twenty years as a teacher, I have never been thus insulted."

This was an imprudent remark.

"Be fair, then!" shouted Bob Hale; and the cry was repeated by others, until the scene of disorder promised to be renewed.

I raised my hand, and shook my head, deprecating the conduct of the boys. Once more they heeded, though it was evidently as a particular favor to me, rather than because it was in keeping with their ideas of right and justice.

"I intend to be fair, young gentlemen," continued Mr. Parasyte; "that is the whole study of my life. I am astonished and mortified at this unlooked-for demonstration. I was about to make a further statement in regard to Thornton, when you interrupted me. I told you that I purposed to give him an opportunity to redeem his character. I intend to do my duty on this painful occasion, though the walls of the Parkville Liberal Institute should crumble above my head, and crush me in the dust."

"Let her crumble!" said a reckless youth, as Mr. Parasyte waxed eloquent.

"Will you be silent, or will you compel me to resort to that which I abhor — to physical force?"

Some of the boys glanced at each other with a

meaning smile when this remark was uttered ; but I shook my head, to signify my disapprobation of anything like resistance or tumult.

"Thornton," added Mr. Parasyte, turning to me, "I have fairly and impartially heard your story, and carefully weighed all your statements. I have come to the conclusion, deliberately and without prejudice, that you were the aggressor."

"I was not, sir," I replied, as gently as I could speak, and yet as firmly.

"It appears that Poodles placed his hand upon your arm merely to attract your attention ; whereupon you struck him a severe blow in the face, which caused him to reel and fall over backward into the lake," said Mr. Parasyte, so pompously that I could not tell whether he intended to "back out" of his position or not.

"Poodles hit me in the head, and was on the point of repeating the blow, when I knocked him over in self-defence."

"It does not appear to me that Poodles, who is a remarkably gentlemanly student, would have struck you for simply refusing to assist him about his examples. Such a course would not be consistent with the character of Poodles."

"No, sir, I did not strike him at any time," protested Poodles.

"I find it impossible to change my opinion of the merits of this case; and for the good of the Parkville Liberal Institute, I must adhere to the sentence I have already — with regret and sorrow — pronounced upon you. But — "

There were again strong signs of another outbreak among the pupils, and I begged them to be silent.

"The conduct of Thornton in this painful emergency merits and receives my approbation. His love of order and his efforts to preserve proper decorum in the school-room are worthy of the highest commendation," continued Mr. Parasyte; "and I would gladly remit the penalty I have imposed upon him without any conditions whatever; but I feel that such a course, after the extraordinary events of this day, would be subversive of the discipline and good order which have ever characterized the Parkville Liberal Institute. I shall, however, impose a merely nominal condition upon Thornton, his compliance with which shall immediately restore him to the full enjoyment of his rights and privileges as a member of this academy. I wish to be as lenient as possible, and, as I observed, the penalty will be merely nominal.

"As the quarrel occurred when the parties were alone, so also may the reparation be made in private; for after Thornton's magnanimous behavior to-day, under these trying circumstances, I do not wish to humiliate or mortify him. I wish that it were consistent with my ideas of stern duty to impose no penalty."

Mr. Parasyte had certainly retreated a long way from his original position. I did not wish to be expelled, and I hailed with satisfaction his manifestation of leniency; and rather than lose the advantages of the school, I was willing to submit to the nominal penalty at which he hinted, supposing it would be a deprivation of some privilege.

"I have not resisted your authority, sir; and I do not mean to do so now," I replied, submissively; for, as the popular sentiment of the students sustained me, I could afford to yield.

4

"Your conduct since the quarrel is entirely satisfactory; I may say that it merits my admiration."
This was toadying to the boys, whom he feared. "I
have sentenced you to expulsion, the severest penalty
known in the discipline of the Parkville Liberal Institute; but, Thornton, I propose to remit this penalty
altogether on condition that, in private, and at your
own convenience, but within one week, you apologize
to Poodles for your conduct. I could not make the
condition any milder, I think."

Mr. Parasyte smiled as though he had entirely
forgiven me; as though he had, in some mysterious
manner, wiped out the stains of falsehood upon my
character. I bowed, but made no reply. I was
sentenced to expulsion; but the penalty was to be
remitted on condition that I would apologize to
Poodles.

Apologize to Poodles! For what? For his attack
upon me, or for the lies he had told about me? It
was no more possible for me to apologize for knocking him over when he assailed me than it would
have been for me to leap across Lake Adieno in the
widest place. I did not wish to deprive myself of

the advantages of attending the Parkville Liberal Institute ; but if my remaining depended upon my humiliating myself before Poodles, upon my declaring that what I had done was wrong, when I believed it was right, I was no longer to be a student in the academy.

The exercises of the school proceeded as usual for a couple of hours, and there were no further signs of insubordination among the boys. At recess I purposely kept away from my more intimate friends, for I did not wish to tell them what course I intended to pursue, fearful that it would renew the disturbance.

An hour before the close of the session, the boys were required to bring in their examination papers in arithmetic. Every student, even to Poodles, handed in solutions to all the problems, and Mr. Parasyte and his assistants at once devoted themselves to the marking of them. In half an hour the principal was ready to report the result.

Half a dozen of the class had all the examples right, and I was one of the number. Very much to my astonishment, Poodles also was announced as one

of the six; and when his name was mentioned, a
score of the students glanced at me.

I did not understand it. I was quite satisfied that
Poodles could not do the problems himself, and it
was certain that he had obtained assistance from
some one, though the declaration on the paper was
duly signed. He had found a friend less scrupulous
than I had been. Some one must have performed
the examples for him; and as he had them all
correct, it was evident that one of the six, who
alone had presented perfect papers, must have afforded the assistance. After throwing out Poodles
and myself, there were but four left; and two of
these, to my certain knowledge, had joined in the
demonstration in my favor: indeed, they were my
friends beyond the possibility of a doubt. Between
the other two I had no means of forming an
opinion.

During the afternoon Mr. Parasyte had been very
uneasy and nervous. It was plain to him that he
ruled the boys by their free will, rather than by his
own power; and this was not a pleasant thing for a
man like him to know. Doubtless he felt that he

had dropped the reins of his team, which, though going very well just then, might take it into its head to run away with him whenever it was convenient. Probably he felt the necessity of doing something to reëstablish his authority, and to obtain a stronger position than that he now occupied. If, with the experience I have since acquired, I could have spoken to him, I should have told him that justice and fairness alone would make him strong as a disciplinarian.

"Poodles," said Mr. Parasyte, just before the close of the session, "I see that all your examples were correctly performed, and that you signed the declaration on the paper."

"Yes, sir," replied Poodles.

"When did you perform them?"

"I did all but two of them last night."

"And when did you do those two?" continued the principal, mildly, but with the air of a man who expects soon to make a triumphant point.

"Between schools, at noon, while the students were at dinner and at play."

4 *

"Very well. You had them all done but two when you met Thornton to-day noon?"

"Yes, sir."

"Thornton," added Mr. Parasyte, turning to me, "I have no disposition to hurry you in the unsettled case of to-day, though the result of Poodles's examination shows that he had no need of the assistance you say he asked of you; but perhaps it would be better that you should state distinctly whether or not you intend to apologize. It is quite possible that there was a misunderstanding between you and Poodles, which a mutual explanation might remove."

"I do not think there was any misunderstanding," I replied.

"If you wish to meet Poodles after school, I offer my services as a friend to assist in the adjustment of the dispute."

"I don't want to meet him," said Poodles.

Mr. Parasyte actually rebuked him for this illiberal sentiment; and while he was doing so, I added that I had no desire to meet Poodles, as proposed. I now think I was wrong; but I had a feeling that the principal intended to browbeat me into an acknowledgment.

"Very well, Thornton; if you refuse to make peace, you must take the consequences. Do you intend to apologize to Poodles, or not?"

"I do not, sir," I replied, decidedly.

"Then you are expelled from the Parkville Liberal Institute."

CHAPTER IV.

IN WHICH ERNEST SAILS THE SPLASH, AND TAKES A BATH.

DIFFICULT as the task was, I had thus far kept cool; but my sentence fell heavily upon me, and I could not help being angry, for I felt that I had been treated unfairly and unjustly. Poodles's statement had been accepted, and mine rejected; his word had been taken, while mine, which ought at least to have passed for as much as his, was utterly disregarded.

I turned upon my heel and went to my seat. My movement was sharp and abrupt, but I did not say anything.

"Stop!" said Mr. Parasyte, who evidently believed that the moment had come for him to vindicate his authority.

I did not stop.

"Stop, I say!" repeated the principal.

I proceeded to pick up my books and papers, to enable me to comply literally with my sentence.

"Come here, Thornton."

I took no notice of the order, but continued to pack up my things.

"Do you hear me?" demanded Mr. Parasyte, in a loud and angry tone.

"I do hear you, sir. I have been expelled, and I don't care about listening to any more speeches."

"If you don't come here, I'll bring you here," added the principal, with emphasis.

Somewhat to my surprise, but greatly to my satisfaction, the boys made no demonstration in my favor. They seemed to think I was now in a mood to fight my own battle, though they were doubtless ready to aid me if I needed any help. Mr. Parasyte appeared to have begun in a way which indicated that he intended to maintain his authority, even at the risk of a personal encounter with me and the boys who had voluntarily espoused my cause.

Having packed up my books and papers, I took the bundle under my arm, and deliberately walked out of the school-room. The principal ordered me to stop; but as he had already sentenced me to expulsion, I could see no reason why I should yield any further allegiance to the magnate of the institution. He was very angry, which was certainly an undignified frame of mind for a gentleman in his position; and I was smarting under the wrong and injustice done to me. Mr. Parasyte stopped to procure his hat, which gave me the advantage in point of time, and I reached the little pier at which my boat was moored before he overtook me.

I hauled in the painter, and pushed off, hoisting the mainsail as the boat receded from the wharf. Mr. Parasyte reached the pier while I was thus engaged.

"Stop, Thornton!" shouted he.

"I would rather not stop any longer," I replied, running up the foresail.

"Will you come back, or I shall bring you back?" demanded he, fiercely.

"Neither, if you please."

"If you wish to save trouble, you will come back," said he.

"I'm not particular about saving trouble. If you have any business with me, I will return."

"I have business with you."

"Will you please to tell me what it is?"

"No, I will not."

"Then you will excuse me if I go home," I added, as I hoisted the jib.

There was only a very light breeze, and the Splash went off very slowly. I took my seat at the helm, trying to keep as cool as possible, though my bosom bounded with emotion. I was playing a strange part, and I was not at home in it. I could not help feeling that I was riding "a high horse;" but the injustice done me seemed to warrant it.

"Poodles, call the men," I heard Mr. Parasyte say to his flunky, and saw him run off to execute the command.

"Once more, Thornton, I ask you to come back," said the principal, still standing on the pier, from which the Splash had receded not more than a couple of rods.

"If you have any business with me, sir, I will do so," I replied. "You have expelled me from the

school, and I don't think you have anything more
to do with me."

"I want no words or arguments. It will be better
for you to come back."

"Perhaps it will; but I shall not come."

There was not breeze enough to enable me to
make a mile an hour, and I had some doubts in
regard to the result, if Mr. Parasyte persisted. He
did persist, and presently Poodles returned with two
men, who were employed upon the school estate, and
whose services were so often required in the boats
that they were good oarsmen. I comprehended the
principal's plan at once. He intended to chase me
in the boat, and bring me back by force. I was
rather amused at the idea, and should have been
more so if there had been a fair sailing breeze.

The Splash was the fastest boat on the lake, or,
at least, faster than any with which I had had an
opportunity to measure paces. But it made but little
difference how fast she was, as long as there was
hardly wind enough to stiffen the mainsail. Mr.
Parasyte ordered the men to take their places on
the thwarts, and ship their oars. I saw that a

little farther out from the shore there was a ripple
on the water, and putting one of my oars out at the
stern, I sculled till I caught the breeze, and the
Splash went off at a little livelier pace.

By this time all the boys had gathered on the
bank of the lake to see the fun, and it *was* fun to
them.   I knew that their sympathies were with me,
and I only wished for a better breeze, that I might
do justice to myself and to my boat.   But the chances
for me were improving as the Splash receded from
the shore.   Mr. Parasyte had taken his place in the
stern sheets of the row-boat, and was urging forward
the men at the oars, who were now pulling with all
their might.   I could not conceal from myself the
fact that they were gaining rapidly upon me.   Unless the wind increased, I should certainly be captured; for the two men with the principal would ask
no better sport than to overhaul and roughly handle
an unruly boy.

But the wind continued to increase as I went
farther out upon the lake, and I soon had all that
was necessary to enable me to keep a "respectful
distance" between the Splash and the row-boat.   By

this time my anger had abated, and I had begun to
enjoy the affair. With a six-knot breeze I could
have it all my own way. I could still see the boys
on the shore, watching the chase with the liveliest
interest and satisfaction. They were not silent ob-
servers, for an occasional cheer or shout was borne
to my ears over the lake, and I could see the waving
of hats, and the swinging of arms, with which my
friends encouraged me to persevere.

Mr. Parasyte was resolute. He felt, doubtless, that
the reputation of the Parkville Liberal Institute, and
his own reputation as a disciplinarian, were at stake.
The tumult in the school-room early in the afternoon would weaken his power and influence over
the boys, unless its effects were counteracted by a
triumph over me. Right or wrong, he probably felt
that he must put me down, or be sacrificed himself;
and he continued to urge his oarsmen forward, intent upon capturing and subduing me.

While I had the breeze I felt perfectly easy. I
had stood out from the shore with the wind on the
beam, and there was nothing to prevent my running
before it directly to the cottage of my uncle. I was

disposed to tantalize my pursuer, and wear out his
men.   I knew that my silent guardian would not
thank me for leading Mr. Parasyte into his presence,
and I was willing to gratify him in this instance.
Besides, the students on the shore seemed to derive too much enjoyment from the scene to have
the sport cut short. Hauling aft the sheets, I stood
down the lake, close to the wind, until I had brought
my pursuer astern of me. I then brought the Splash
up into the wind, and coolly waited for the row-boat
to come up within hailing distance.

Mr. Parasyte, deceived by my position, thought his
time had come.   He was much excited, and with
renewed zeal pressed his oarsmen to increase their
efforts. When he had approached within a few rods
of me, I put up the helm, and dashed away again
towards the pier.   Again I distanced him, and ran
as near to the pier as I dared to go, fearful that I
might lose the wind under the lee of a bluff below
the school grounds. The boys hailed me with a
cheer, which must have been anything but soothing
to the feelings of Mr. Parasyte.   Then, "wing and
wing," I ran off before the wind; and, still unwilling

to deprive my friends of the excitement of witnessing the race, I again stood out towards the middle of the lake.

The principal could not give up the pursuit without abandoning the high position he had taken, and subjecting himself to the derision of the students. He followed me, therefore, and I led him over the same course he had gone before. On my return I unfortunately ran in a little too near the shore, and got under the lee of the bluff, which nearly becalmed me. I realized that I had made a fatal blunder, and I wished I had disappointed the boys, and continued on my course across the lake, where the wind favored me. I tried to scull the Splash out of the still water before Mr. Parasyte came up.

"Pull with all your might, men!" said the principal, excitedly; and they certainly did so.

Seeing that he was upon me, I attempted to come about, and run off before the wind; but I had lost my steerage-way. I suppose I was somewhat "flurried" by the danger of my situation, and did not do as well as I might have done.

"Pull! Pull!" shouted Mr. Parasyte, nervously, as he steered the row-boat.

Thus urged, the men did pull better than I had ever known them to do before. The principal of the Parkville Liberal Institute was no boatman himself, and his calculations were miserably deficient, or else his intentions were more vicious than I had given him credit for. He was angry and excited; and as I looked at him, it seemed to me that he did not know what he was about. The Splash lay broadside to him. She was a beautiful craft, built light and graceful, rather than strong and substantial. On the other hand, the row-boat was a solid, sharp, ram-nosed craft, setting low in the water; and on it came at the highest speed to which it could be urged by the powerful muscles of the strong men at the oars.

"Pull! Pull!" repeated Mr. Parasyte, fiercely, under the madness of the excitement and the resentment caused by the hard chase I had led him.

"Down with your helm, or you will smash me!" I shouted, seeing that a collision was inevitable.

If Mr. Parasyte did not intend to run me down, my warning was too late. The row-boat came upon me like a whirlwind, striking the Splash on the

5 *

CHAPTER V.

IN WHICH ERNEST DECLINES A PROPOSITION.

THE battle had been fought and lost to me. Mr. Parasyte, roused to the highest pitch of anger and excitement, seemed to be determined to overwhelm me. He was reckless and desperate. He had smashed my boat apparently with as little compunction as he would snap a dead stick in his fingers. He was thoroughly in earnest now; and it was fully demonstrated that he intended to protect the discipline of the Parkville Liberal Institute, even if it cost a human life for him to do so.

I was then "lying round loose" in the lake. I had no idea that I was in any personal peril from the water; all that disturbed me was the fact that I could not swim fast enough to keep out of the principal's way. The treacherous breeze had deserted me in the midst of my triumph, and consigned me to the tender mercies of my persecutor.

I swam away from the boat which had been pursuing me, as though from an instinct which prompted me to escape my oppressor; but Mr. Parasyte, without giving any attention to my sinking craft, ordered his men to pull again; and he steered towards me. Of course a few strokes enabled him to overtake me. If I had had the means, I would have resisted even then, and avoided capture; for I could easily have swum ashore. But it would have been childish for me to hold out any longer; and when one of the men held out his oar to me, I grasped it, and was assisted into the boat.

"Are you satisfied, Thornton?" said Mr. Parasyte, with a sneer, as I shook myself like a water dog, and took my seat in the boat.

"No, sir; I am not satisfied," I replied.

"What are you going to do about it?'

"I don't know about that; I will see in due time."

"You will see in due time, I trust, that the discipline of the Parkville Liberal Institute is not to be set at defiance with impunity."

"I have not set the discipline at defiance. I submitted myself, and did what I could to make others do so. You can't say that I did anything wrong while I was a member of the academy. You turned me out, and I was going quietly and in order, when you began to browbeat me."

"I ordered you to come to me, and you did not come. That was downright disobedience."

"It was after you had turned me out; and all I had to do was to go."

"You were still on my premises, and were subject to my orders."

"I don't think I was."

"I shall not argue the matter with you. I am going to teach you the duty of obedience."

"Perhaps you will; but I don't believe you will," I replied, in a tone of defiance.

"We'll see."

"There's another thing we'll see, while we are about it; and that is, you will pay for smashing my boat."

"Pay for it!" exclaimed he.

"I think so."

"I think not."

"You will, if there is any law in the land."

"Law!" ejaculated he; but his lips actually quivered with anger at the idea of such an outrage upon his magnificent dignity, as being sued, and compelled in a court of justice to pay for the boat he had destroyed.

"You had no right to run into my boat—no more right than I had to set your house on fire."

"We will see."

He relapsed into a dignified silence; but he was thinking, I fancy, how very pleasant it would be for him to pay three or four hundred dollars for the Splash; not that he would care much for the money, but it would make him appear so ridiculous in the eyes of the students.

The men were pulling for the shore; but I observed that Mr. Parasyte did not head the boat towards the pier, where the boys were waiting our return. Probably he feared that they would attempt to resist his mighty will, and deliver me from his hands. He intended, therefore, to land farther down the lake, and convey me to the Institute buildings by some unfrequented way.

For my own part, I was not much disturbed by Mr. Parasyte's intentions or movements. The only thing that really distressed me was the loss of my boat; for the Splash had been one of my best and dearest friends. I was a little sentimental in regard to her; and her destruction gave me a pang of keen regret akin to anguish. I had cruised all over the lake in her; had eaten and slept in her for a week at a time, and I actually loved her. She was worthy to be loved, for she had served me faithfully in storm and sunshine. It is quite likely that I had some feelings of revenge towards the tyrant who had crushed her, and I was thinking how he could be compelled to pay for the damage he had done.

As soon as I had, in a measure, recovered my equanimity, I tried to obtain the bearings of the spot where the Splash had disappeared beneath the waters, so that, if I failed to obtain justice, I might possibly recover my boat. If raised, she was in very bad condition; for her side was stove in, and I feared she could not be repaired so as to be as good as she was before.

As the row-boat neared the shore, I made my preparations to escape from my captor; for it was not my intention to be borne back in triumph to the Institute, as a sacrifice to the violated discipline of the establishment. When the boat touched the beach, I meant to jump into the water, and thus pass the men, who were too powerful for me. I changed my position so as to favor my purpose; but Mr. Parasyte had been a schoolmaster too many years not to comprehend the thought which was passing through my mind. He picked up the boat-hook, and it was clear to me that he intended with this instrument to prevent my escape.

The boat was beached; but I saw no good chance to execute my purpose, and was forced to wait till circumstances favored me. The spot where we had put in was over two miles distant from the Institute by the road, though not more than one by water. Mr. Parasyte directed one of the men to go to a stable, near the shore, and procure a covered carriage, compelling me to keep my seat in the stern of the boat near him, while the messenger was absent. He still held the boat-hook in his hand, with which he could fasten to me if I made any movement.

When the vehicle came, the principal placed me on the back seat, and took position himself at my side. One of the men was to drive, while the other was directed to await his return, and then pull the boat back. I was forced to acknowledge to myself that Mr. Parasyte's strategy was excellent, and that I was completely baffled by it; but as I was satisfied that my time would soon come, I was content to submit, with what patience I could command, to the captivity from which I could not escape.

The vehicle was driven to the front door of the Institute; and the boys, who were still on the shore of the lake, watching for the return of the boat, did not have any notice of the arrival of the prisoner. I was conducted to the hall of the principal's apartments first, and then to a vacant chamber on the third floor. Mr. Parasyte performed this duty himself, being unwilling to intrust my person to the care of one his subordinate teachers. A suit of clothes belonging to a boy of my own

size was sent to me, and I was directed to put
it on, while my own dress was dried at the laun-
dry fire. This was proper and humane, and I did
not object.

When I had changed my clothing, Mr. Parasyte
presented himself. By this time he had thoroughly cooled off. He looked solemn and dignified as
he entered the little room, and seated himself in
one of the two chairs, which, with the bed, formed
the furniture of the apartment. He had probably
considered the whole subject of his relations with
me, and was now prepared to give his final decision, to which I was also prepared to listen.

"Thornton," said he, with a kind of jerk in his
voice.

"Sir."

"You have made more trouble in the Parkville
Liberal Institute to-day than all the other boys
together have made since the establishment was
founded."

"I didn't make it," I replied, promptly, intending
to give him an early assurance that I would not
recede from the position I had taken.

"Yes, you did. You provoked a quarrel, and refused to apologize — a very mild penalty for the
offence you had committed."

"I deny that I provoked a quarrel, sir."

"That question has been settled, and we will not
open it again. I have shown the students, by my
prompt pursuit of you when you set my authority
at defiance, that I intended to maintain the discipline of this institution. I have taken you and
brought you back. So far I am satisfied, Thornton."

"I am not. You have smashed my boat, and
you must pay for her," I added, calmly, but in the
most uncompromising manner.

"This is not a matter of dollars and cents with
me. I would rather have given a thousand dollars
than had this trouble occur; and I would give
half that sum now to have it satisfactorily settled."

Mr. Parasyte wiped his brow, for he was thrown
into a violent perspiration by the mental effort
which this acknowledgment caused him. It looked
like "backing out."

"Thornton, you are a very popular young man
among the students; it would be useless to deny

it, if I were disposed to do so. You have the sympathies of your companions, because Poodles is not popular."

"The boys don't like Poodles simply because he is not a good fellow. He is a liar and a cheat, and —"

"Nothing more of that kind need be said. What I have done cannot be undone."

"Very well, sir; I have been expelled. Let me go; that's all I ask."

"In due time you will have permission to go. I think I am, technically, legally liable for the destruction of your boat," he added, wiping his brow again; for it was hard work for him to say so much. "But you have defied me, and the well-being of this institution required that I should act promptly. I wish to make a proposition to you."

He paused and looked at me. I intimated that I was ready to hear him.

"In about an hour the boys will assemble for evening prayers," he continued, after rising from his chair and consulting his watch. "If at that time you will apologize to me for your conduct, in their presence, and before that time to Poodles, privately, I will restore you to your rank and privileges in the Parkville Liberal Institute, and — and pay you for your boat."

"I will not do it, sir," I replied, without an instant's hesitation.

Mr. Parasyte gave me a glance of mingled anger and mortification, and turning on his heel, left the room, locking the door upon me.

6*

CHAPTER VI.

IN WHICH ERNEST FINDS HIS FELLOW-STUDENTS
IN OPEN REBELLION.

TO apologize to Poodles was to acknowledge that I had done wrong. Had I done wrong so far as my fellow-student was concerned? Seriously and earnestly I asked myself this question. No; I had told the truth in regard to the affair exactly as it was, and it would be a lie for me to apologize to Poodles. I could not and would not do it. I would be cut to pieces, and have my limbs torn piecemeal from my body before I would do it.

As far as the principal was concerned, I felt that, provoked and irritated by his tyranny and injustice, I had exhibited a proud and defiant spirit, which was dangerous to the discipline of the school: I was sorry that, when he called me back, I had not obeyed. While I was in the school-room, or on the premises of the academy, I should have yielded obedience, both in fact and in spirit; and I could not excuse my defiant bearing by the plea that I had been expelled. I was willing, after reflection, to apologize to Mr. Parasyte.

He proposed to pay for my boat. This was a great concession on his part, though it was called forth by the belief that he was legally liable for its destruction. He was willing to do me justice in that respect, if I would humiliate myself before Poodles, and publicly heal the wound which the discipline of the Institute had received at my hands. Even at that time it seemed to me to be noble and honorable to acknowledge an error and atone for it; and I am quite sure, if I could have felt that I had done wrong, I should have been glad to own it, and to make the confession in the presence of the students. There was a principle at stake, and something more than mere personal feeling.

While I was debating with myself what I should do, Mr. Parasyte appeared again. It was a matter of infinite importance to him. The prosperity, if not the very existence, of his school depended upon the issue of this affair; and he was naturally nervous and excited. The students were in a state of incipient rebellion, as their conduct in the afternoon indicated, and it was of the highest moment to the Institute to have the matter amicably adjusted.

On the one hand, if I apologized to Poodles and the principal, the "powers that be" would be vindicated, and the authority of the master fully established. On the other hand, if I declined to do so, and the sentence of expulsion was carried out, the boys were in sympathy with me, and the rebellion might break out afresh, and end in the total dissolution of the establishment. Under these circumstances, it was not strange that Mr. Parasyte desired to see me again.

"I hope you have carefully considered your position, Thornton," said he.

"I have," I replied; "and I am willing to apologize to you, but not to Poodles."

"That is something gained," added he; and I could see his face brighten up under the influence of a hope.

"My manner was defiant, and my conduct disobedient. I am willing to apologize to you for this, and to submit to such punishment as you think proper to inflict."

"That is very well; but it does not fully meet the difficulty. You must also apologize to Poodles, which you are aware may be done in private."

"I cannot do it, sir, either in public or in private. Poodles was wholly and entirely to blame."

"I think not; when I settled the case it was closed up, and it must not be opened again; at least not till some new testimony is obtained. I cannot eat my own words."

"You may obtain new testimony, if you desire," I suggested.

"What?"

"Poodles signed the declaration that he had performed the examples on the papers without assistance."

"He did. Have you any doubt that such is the case?" asked Mr. Parasyte, though he must have been satisfied that Poodles did not work out the examples.

"I am entirely confident that he did not perform them. Mr. Parasyte," I continued, earnestly, "I desire to stay at the Institute. It would be very bad for me to be turned out, and I am willing to confess I have done wrong. If you give Poodles the paper with the examination on it, and he can perform one half of the examples, even now, without help, I will apologize to him in public or in private."

"That looks very fair, but it is not," replied the principal, rubbing his head, as if to stimulate his ideas.

"If Poodles can do the problems, I shall be willing to believe that I am mistaken. In my opinion, he cannot perform a single one of them, let alone the whole of them."

"I object to this proceeding," said he, impatiently. "It will be equivalent to my making a confession."

The bell rang for the boys to assemble for the evening devotions. It gave Mr. Parasyte a shock, for the business was still unsettled. I had submitted to him a method by which he could ascertain the truth or falsehood of Poodle's statements; but it involved an acknowledgment that he, Mr. Parasyte, was in the wrong. He seemed to be afraid it would be proved that he had made a blunder; that he had given an unjust judgment. I was fully aware that the principal's position was a difficult and painful one, and I was even disposed to sympathize with him to a certain extent, though I was the victim of his partiality and injustice. The perils and discomforts of his situation, however, had been produced by his own hasty and unfair judgment; and it would have been far better for him even to apologize to me. He would have lost nothing with the boys by such a course; for never in my life did I have so exalted an opinion of a schoolmaster, as when, conscious that he had done wrong, he nobly and magnanimously acknowledged his error, and begged the forgiveness of the boy whom he had unintentionally misjudged.

I feel bound to say, in this connection, and after a longer experience of the world, that many schoolmasters, " armed with a little brief authority," are the most contemptible of petty tyrants. Their arrogance and oppression are intolerable; and I have often wondered, that where such men have been planted, they have not produced more of the evil fruit of strife and rebellion.   Mr. Parasyte was one of this class; and the fact that he was a splendid teacher did not help his influence in the slightest degree.

"There is the bell for evening prayers, Thornton, and it is necessary for me to know instantly what you intend to do," said the principal.

"I shall not apologize to Poodles; I will to you."

"Think well of it."

"I have done so.   If Poodles can do one half the examples on the paper, I will apologize."

"I have decided that question, and shall not open it again."

"I have nothing more to say, Mr. Parasyte," I replied, with becoming dignity, as I braced myself for the consequences of the decision I had made.

"You are an obstinate and self-willed fellow!" exclaimed the principal, irritated by the result.

I made no reply.

"The consequences be upon your own head."

I bowed in silence.

"You have lost your good character and your boat."

I glanced out of the window, and saw the boys filing into the school-room.

"I shall explain this matter to your fellow-students, and tell them what I proposed."

"Do so," I answered.

He could not help seeing that I was thoroughly in earnest, and that I did not intend to yield any more than I had indicated. He was vexed, annoyed, angry, and bolted out of the room, at last, in no proper frame of mind to conduct the religious exercises of the hour. It was quite dark now; and I lay down upon the bed, to think of what had passed, and to conjecture the result of my conduct. How I sighed then for some kind friend to advise me! How I wished that I had a father who would tell me what to do, and fight my battle for me! How I longed for a tender mother, into whose loving face I could gaze as I related the sad experience of that eventful day! Perhaps she would bid me apologize to Poodles, for the sake of saving my good name, and retaining my con-

7

nection with the school. If so, though it would be weak and unworthy, I could humble myself for her sake.

I felt that I had done right. I had made all the concession which truth and justice required of me, and I was quite calm. I hardly inquired why Mr. Parasyte was keeping me a prisoner in the Institute after he had expelled me, or what he intended to do with me. About nine o'clock my own clothes were brought back to me by one of the servants; but the door was securely locked when he retired.

A few minutes later, and before the sound of the servant's retreating footsteps had ceased, I heard some one thrust a key into the door. It did not fit, and a dozen others were tried in like manner, but with no better success. I heard a whispered consultation; and then the door began to strain, and crack, until the bolt yielded, and it flew open. My sympathizing friends, the students, headed by Bob Hale, had broken it down.

"Come, Ernest," said Bob. "You needn't stay in here any longer. We want you down stairs."

" What are you going to do?" I asked, quietly, of my excited deliverers.

"There is no law or justice in this concern; and we are going to put things to rights," replied Tom Rush, a good fellow, who had spent a week's vacation with me circumnavigating Lake Adieno in the Splash.

" You know I don't approve of any rows or riots," I added.

"No row nor riot about it. We have taken possession of this establishment, and we are going to straighten things out, — you can bet your life on that."

" Where is Mr. Parasyte?"

" He has gone up to see your uncle. He told us, at evening prayers, what an obstinate boy you were; how kind, and tender, and forgiving he had been to you, and how he had exhausted good nature in trying to bring you to a proper sense of duty."

" Did he say that?"

" He did, and much more. But come with us. The fellows have captured the citadel, and we hold the school-room now, waiting for you."

"I will go with you; but I don't want the fellows to make a disturbance."

"No disturbance at all, Ernest; but we have turned the assistant teachers out, and mean to ascertain who is right and who is wrong in this matter."

The rebellion had actually broken out again; and the students, in the most high-handed manner, had established a tribunal in the school-room, to try the issue of my affair with the principal. I followed Bob Hale, Tom Rush, and half a dozen others, who constituted the committee to wait on me. They conducted me to the main school-room, which was a large hall. At every door and window were stationed two or three of the larger boys, with their hockies, bats, and rulers as weapons, to defend the court, as they called it, from any interruption.

About two thirds of the students were there assembled; and though the gathering was a riotous proceeding, the boys were in as good order as during the sessions of the school. In an arm-chair, on the platform, sat Henry Vallington, one of the oldest and most dignified students of the Institute, who, it appeared, was to act as judge. Before him were Bill Poodles and Dick Pearl, — the latter being one of the six whose examples were all right, — arraigned for trial, and guarded by four stout students.

7 *

CHAPTER VII.

IN WHICH ERNEST ATTENDS THE TRIAL OF BILL
POODLES AND DICK PEARL.

I CONFESS that I was appalled at the boldness and daring of my fellow-students, who had
actually taken possession of the Parkville Liberal
Institute, and purposed to mete out justice to me
and to Bill Poodles. There was a certain kind
of solemnity in the proceedings, which was not
without its effect upon me. My companions were
thoroughly in earnest, and the affair was not to be
a farce.

Mr. Parasyte, after prayer, had made a statement
to the students in regard to the unpleasant event
of the day, in which he represented me as a con-
tumacious offender, one who desired to make all
the trouble he could; an obstinate, self-willed fellow, whose example was dangerous to the general

peace, and who had refused to be guided by reason and common sense. He told the students that
he had even offered to pay for my boat — a concession on his part which had had no effect in soft-
ening my obdurate nature. He appealed to them to
sustain the discipline of the Parkville Liberal Institute, which had always been celebrated as a remarkably orderly and quiet establishment. He then
added that he should consult my uncle in regard
to me, and be guided in some measure by his judgment.

The students heard him in silence; but Bob Hale
assured me that it was with compressed lips, and
a fixed determination to carry out the plan which
had been agreed upon while the boys were watching the chase on the lake, and which had not been
modified by the wilful destruction of the Splash.

I glanced around at my fellow-students as I entered the hall; and though they smiled as their
gaze met mine, there was a look of earnestness and
determination which could not be mistaken. Henry
Vallington, the chairman, judge, or whatever the
name of his office was, had the reputation of being

the steadiest boy in the school. It was understood that he intended to become a minister. He was about eighteen, and was nearly fitted to enter college. He never joined in what were called the "scrapes" of the Institute, but devoted himself with the closest attention to his studies. He was esteemed and respected by all who knew him; and when I saw him presiding over this irregular assemblage, I could not help regarding the affair as much more serious than it had before seemed, even to me, the chief actor therein.

Poodles and Pearl, I learned, had been captured in their rooms, and dragged by sheer force into the school-room, to be examined on the charges to be preferred against them. Poodles looked timid and terrified, while Pearl was dogged and resolute.

"Thornton," said Henry Vallington, as my conductors paused before the judge, "I have sent for you in order that we may ascertain the truth of the charges brought against you by Mr. Parasyte. If you provoked the quarrel to-day noon with Poodles, it is no more than fair and right that you should make the apology required of you. If you did not, we intend to stand by you. Have you anything to say?"

"I wish to say, in the first place, that, guilty or innocent, I am willing to submit to whatever penalty the principal imposes upon me."

"That is very well for you, but it won't do for us," interposed the judge. "If such gross injustice is done to one, it may be to another. We act in self-defence."

"I don't know what you intend to do; but I am opposed to any disorderly conduct, and to any violation of the rules of the Institute."

"We know you are, Thornton; and you shall not be held responsible for what we do to-night. If you are willing to tell us what you know about this affair, all right. If not, we shall go on without you."

"I am willing to tell the truth here, as I have done to-day. As there seems to be some mistake in regard to what transpired between Mr. Parasyte and myself, up stairs, I will state the facts as they occurred. He agreed to pay for my boat on condition that I would apologize, privately, to Poodles,

and publicly to the principal. I offered to apologize
to Mr. Parasyte, but not to Poodles, who was the
aggressor in the beginning. I told him, if Poodles
would perform half the examples now, I would make
the apology to him.

"That's it!" shouted half a dozen boys.

"Order!" interposed the judge, sternly.

"I think that would be a good way to prove that
Poodles did or did not tell the truth, when he
said he had performed the examples," interposed
Bob Hale.

"Capital!" added Tom Rush.

"I approve the method; but let us have no disorder," replied Vallington. "Conduct Poodles to the
blackboard."

The custodians of the culprit promptly obeyed this
order, and led him to the blackboard, which was
cleaned for immediate use. The school-room was
well lighted, and the expression on the faces of
all could be distinctly seen.

"Poodles, we desire to have justice done to all,"
said Vallington, when the culprit had taken his
place at the blackboard. "You shall have fair play

in every respect. You shall have a chance to prove that you were right, and Thornton wrong."

"Well, I was right," replied Poodles.

"Did you perform all the examples on your paper without any help?"

"Of course I did."

"Then of course you know how to perform them. Here is an examination paper. If you can perform five of the ten examples you shall be acquitted."

"Perhaps I don't choose to do them," said Poodles, looking around for some way to escape his fate.

"Are you not willing that the truth should come out?"

"I told the truth to-day."

"All right, if you did. You surely will not object to *prove* that you did. You shall have fair play, I repeat."

"Suppose I don't choose to do them?" asked Poodles, doubtfully.

"Then we shall take it for granted that you did not do them, as you declared on your paper."

"You can take it for granted, then, if you like," answered Poodles, as he dropped the chalk.

"You refuse to perform the examples — do you?" demanded Vallington, sternly.

"Yes, I do."

"Then you may take the consequences. Either you shall be expelled from the Institute, or at least fifty of us will petition our parents to take us from this school. We have done with you."

Bill Poodles smiled, and was pleased to get off so easily; but I noticed that Dick Pearl turned pale, and looked very much troubled. He was a relative of Mr. Parasyte, and it was generally understood that he was a free scholar, his parents being too poor to pay his board and tuition. While he expected to be ducked in the lake, or subjected to some personal indignity, after the manner in which boys usually treat such cases, his courage was good. Now, it appeared that the boys simply intended to have Poodles expelled, or to ask their parents and guardians to remove them; and as most of the students were from fourteen to eighteen years of age, they would probably have influence enough to effect their design.

"Pearl," said the judge, while the other culprit was apparently still attempting to figure out the result of the trial.

"I'm here," replied Pearl.

"We are entirely satisfied that Poodles had some assistance in performing his examples. It is believed that you gave him that assistance. If you did, own up."

"Who says I helped Poodles?"

"I say so, for one," added the judge, sharply.

"Can you prove it?"

"I will answer that question after you have confessed or refused to confess. You shall have fair play, as well as Poodles. If you wish to put yourself right on the record, you can do so; if not, you shall leave, or we will."

Pearl looked troubled. He was under very great obligations to Mr. Parasyte. If he denied that he had helped Poodles, and it was then proved against him, the boys would insist that he should be expelled. If he stood out, he must either be expelled or the Institute be broken up. He did not appear willing to take such a responsibility.

8

"You can do as you please, Pearl; but tell the truth, if you say anything," continued Vallington."

"I did help Poodles," said he, looking down at the floor.

"How much did you help him?"

"I lent him my examination paper, and he copied all the solutions upon his own."

"And after that you were willing to declare that you had not assisted any one?" demanded the judge, with a look of supreme contempt on his fine features.

"I had not helped any one *when* I signed my paper."

"Humph!" exclaimed Vallington, with a withering sneer. "That is the meanest kind of a lie."

"I didn't mean to assist him; he teased me till I couldn't help myself," pleaded Pearl.

A further examination showed that Poodles had browbeaten and threatened him; and we were disposed to palliate Pearl's offence, in consideration of his poverty and his dependent position, after he had confessed his error.

"Are you willing to make this acknowledgment

to Mr. Parasyte?" asked the judge, in a tone of compassion.

"I don't want to; but I will. I suppose he will send me home then," replied the culprit.

"We will do what we can for you," added the judge.

Pearl had been a pretty good fellow among the boys, was generally popular, and all were sorry for him. But his confession in a manner absolved him, and the students heartily declared that they would stand by him.

"Our business is finished," said Vallington, "unless Poodles has something more to say."

Poodles had listened with consternation to the confession of Pearl, and he now appeared to be dissatisfied with himself rather than with the court.

"I didn't think Dick Pearl would let on in that way," said he, casting a reproachful glance at his fellow-culprit.

"He has told the truth. If he had not confessed, we could have proved that he helped you," added Vallington. "I have seen the six papers that were all right myself. Pearl performed the third example in a very peculiar and roundabout way; and Poodles had it in the same way, while he did the other four by the most direct method."

"I suppose it's of no use to stand out now," said Poodles, timidly.

"Will you confess now?"

"I will, if it will do any good."

"If you will tell the truth to Mr. Parasyte, that is all we want. The fellows haven't anything against you. Will you do so?"

"I will if you say I shall not be expelled," whined Poodles.

"I can only say that we will not ask for your expulsion. I suppose there is no danger of Mr. Parasyte expelling *you*," added the judge, with a dry humor, appreciated by all the students.

"Mr. Parasyte!" exclaimed one of the sentinels at the door.

There was an attempt on the part of the principal to pull the door open, but it was well secured upon the inside.

"Let him in," said the judge.

The door opened, and Mr. Parasyte entered the school-room.

CHAPTER VIII.

IN WHICH ERNEST VANQUISHES THE SCHOOLMASTER.

MR. PARASYTE had evidently obtained some information in regard to the great rebellion before he entered the school-room; for though he looked extremely troubled, he did not seem to be so much astonished as might have been expected. He was admitted by order of the judge, and took off his hat as he walked up the aisle to the platform, wiping away the perspiration which gathered on his heated brow under the severe mental struggles his position induced.

"What does all this mean?" he demanded, with a sternness which we could not help seeing was assumed.

The boys were all orderly and quiet; the school-room was as still as during the regular sessions of the Institute. The sentinels, with their bats and

8 *

clubs, stood immovable at their stations, and the scene produced its full impression upon the mind of the principal. As he did not seem to be prepared to receive an answer to his question, none was given; and Mr. Parasyte glanced uneasily around the room, apparently seeking to obtain a better understanding of the scene.

"What does all this *mean?*" demanded he, a second time.

"It means, sir," replied Henry Vallington, "that the boys are dissatisfied, and intend to have things set right."

"Is this a proper way to express their dissatisfaction — to take advantage of my absence to get up a riotous assembly ? "

"We have been perfectly orderly, sir," added the judge, in respectful tones.

"How came you here, Thornton?" continued the principal, as his gaze rested on me.

"We brought him here, sir," promptly interposed Vallington, anxious to relieve me of any responsibility for my escape from my prison-chamber.

"Vallington, I confess my astonishment at seeing

you engaged in an affair of this kind," said Mr. Parasyte, reproachfully; and he fixed his gaze upon the judge, and again wiped the perspiration from his forehead. "I have always regarded you as an orderly and well-behaved boy."

"I do not expect to forfeit my reputation as such by what I have done. Mr. Parasyte, the boys are dissatisfied. We are not little children. We have all reached the years of discretion, and we know the difference between right and wrong, between justice and injustice."

"Do you intend to read me a lecture?" demanded the principal, angrily.

"No, sir; I had no such intention — only to state the facts."

"But you are arraigning me, the principal of the Parkville Liberal Institute," added Mr. Parasyte, measuring the judge from head to foot.

"You may call it what you please, sir."

"May I ask what you purpose to do?" continued the principal, in a sneering tone, not unmingled with timidity.

"Poodles," said the judge, turning to the lank toady, "stand up."

He obeyed; and being now with the majority of the boys, I think he was mean enough to enjoy the discomfiture of Mr. Parasyte, for there can be no real respect or true sympathy in the relation of one flunky with another.

"Are you ready to tell the whole truth?" demanded Vallington.

"I am," replied Poodles.

"Perhaps you will be willing to inform Mr. Parasyte, in the beginning, whether you do so of your own free will and accord, or not."

"I do so of my own free will and accord."

"Did you perform the examples on the examination paper without any assistance?"

"I did not."

"How many did you do yourself?"

"None of them."

"Who struck the first blow in the affray on the pier with Thornton?"

"I did," answered Poodles, with a silly leer. "Thornton told the facts just exactly as they were."

"You may sit down."

Mr. Parasyte wiped his brow again.

"Pearl," continued Vallington.

This culprit, unlike his companion in guilt, looked sheepish and crestfallen, as he slowly rose from his seat. He was not so base and low-minded as Poodles, and he felt a genuine shame for the mean conduct of which he had been guilty.

"Have you anything to say, Pearl?" asked the judge.

"I lent my paper to Poodles, who copied the solutions from it," replied Pearl, with his glance fixed upon the floor.

"That's all; you may sit down."

Pearl seated himself; and if a pin had fallen to the floor then, it might have been heard in the anxious silence that followed. Mr. Parasyte's chest heaved with emotion. He wanted to storm, and scold, and threaten, but seemed to be afraid to do so.

"I have nothing more to say at present, Mr. Parasyte. In the name and in behalf of the students, I have brought the facts to your notice," said Vallington, breaking the impressive stillness, as the principal did not seem disposed to do so.

"After the riotous proceedings of this afternoon, I might have expected this; but I did not," the principal began. "You appear to have intimidated Poodles to such an extent that he has entirely modified and reversed the statements he made this afternoon. He is a weak-minded boy, and it was not difficult to do so.".

This remark roused the ire of Poodles, and it required a sharp reprimand from the judge to repress his impertinence.

"Pearl is a poor boy, upon whose fears you seem to have successfully wrought. A confession from either of them, under the circumstances, is not reliable. I do not countenance this meeting, or these proceedings. I am not to be intimidated by your action. In regard to what you have done, I have nothing to say; but I require you to separate, and go at once to your rooms."

"Will you be kind enough to inform us what you intend to do, Mr. Parasyte?" said Vallington.

"I am not to be taken to task by my pupils."

"We do not intend to resort to any disorderly proceedings," added the judge. "Poodles and Pearl, without compulsion, have acknowledged their errors, and it has been fully proved that Thornton was not to blame for the affair on the pier. We ask, therefore, that Thornton be restored to his rank and privileges as a member of the Institute. If this is not done, at least fifty of us will sign a paper urging our parents and guardians to take us away from this school."

"I will grant nothing under these circumstances — promise nothing," replied the principal, doggedly.

"We are in no haste. We leave the matter for your consideration, Mr. Parasyte. We will all go to our rooms now."

Vallington left the chair, and walked out of the school-room, followed in good order by all the students who had taken part in these irregular proceedings. I was going out with the rest, when Mr. Parasyte intimated that he had something to say to me, and I remained. When the boys had all gone, he invited me to accompany him to his private office — a small apartment, opening from the main hall, near the front door, in which he received callers, and sat in state when not employed in the school-room.

There is an old saying that "you must summer and winter" a man before you know him. Mr. Parasyte was considered a tyrant; not a coarse and brutal tyrant, but a refined and gentlemanly one, who cows you by his polite impertinence. He seldom indulged in harsh speech, never in personal violence — at least no instance of it was known to the students. He indulged in sneers and polished browbeating. A boy was never stupid — he lacked common intelligence; never a blockhead — his perceptions were very dull. His polite epithets were more cutting than good round invectives would have been.

He had a will of his own; and he was obstinate, mulish, pig-headed. If he had been surprised into declaring that black was white, then black would continue to be white, in spite of positive demonstration to the contrary. He was dogmatic to the last degree; and this is a fault to which the schoolmaster is peculiarly liable. It required the event of the day whereof I speak to enable us fully to comprehend Mr. Parasyte. We had summered him before; now we were to winter him.

What he had said in the school-room indicated that he intended to regard the confessions of Poodles and Pearl as extorted from them by intimidation, and that he purposed to persist in persecuting me. I had no desire to be a martyr; but I did not see how I could help myself.

"Thornton, I see you intend, if possible, to break up the Parkville Liberal Institute," said he.

"No, sir, I do not. I hadn't anything to do with what took place in the school-room," I replied.

"You did not seem to be a martyr there," sneered he. "The boys have made a mistake; so have you. They don't know me; you don't. You got up a quarrel this afternoon."

"No, sir, I did not."

"Don't contradict me," said he, sharply. "I say you got up a quarrel this afternoon."

"And I say I did not."

"I am in no humor to trifle with you," said he, opening a desk, and taking out a cowhide.

I was willing to confess, when I saw that implement, that I had not known him before. He was about to step down from refined to brutal tyranny.

9

"Poodles himself has confessed that he lied," I added, taking no further notice of the cowhide.

"Confessed!" exclaimed Mr. Parasyte, savagely. "The boys have either bribed or frightened him into this confession. It will have no effect upon me."

"I have nothing to say, then," I answered, with dignity. "If you will look into the case again, and require Poodles to do the examples, you will see that you, and not the boys, have made a mistake."

"Silence, sir! I don't intend to be addressed in that impudent way by any student. I have attempted to suppress this rebellion by mild means; but they have failed. I have been to see your uncle. As I supposed he would, he has taken a proper view of the case. He does not wish to have you expelled, and I revoke my sentence; but he desires to have you reduced to subjection."

My uncle had actually spoken, and taken sides with the tyrant. I was astonished, but not intimidated.

"I have drawn up a paper for you to sign, which shall be read to the boys to-morrow morning. There it is."

RESISTANCE TO TYRANNY. — Page 99.

I glanced at the document. It was an acknowledgment of all Mr. Parasyte charged me with, and a promise to behave myself properly. I refused to sign it. The principal rolled up his sleeves, and took the cowhide in his hand. He looked cool and malignant.

"Then I shall do as your uncle wishes me to do — reduce you to subjection," said he. "Consider well what you are doing."

"I have considered, sir. If you strike me with that cowhide, I shall do the best I can to defend myself."

"Do you threaten me?" demanded Mr. Parasyte, stepping towards me with a jerk.

"No, sir; but I will not submit to a blow, if it costs me my life."

"Won't you? We'll see."

He did see. He struck me. The blow cut my soul. I sprang upon him with all the tiger in my nature let loose. I kicked, bit, scratched. I clawed at his throat like a vampire, and, though severely belabored, I finally wrenched the cowhide from his grasp, and hurled him back so that he fell full length upon the floor.

CHAPTER IX.

IN WHICH ERNEST STRIKES A HEAVY BLOW, AND WINS ANOTHER VICTORY.

I WAS astonished at my own prowess, as I stood, with heaving breast, gazing at the prostrate form of the vanquished tyrant. I was a stout young fellow, heavy enough and strong enough for a boy of fifteen; but I did not regard myself as a match for a full-grown man. I suppose the fury and impetuosity of the onslaught I made had given me the victory before Mr. Parasyte was able to bring all his power to bear upon me.

I was satisfied with what I had done, and did not care to do any more. I wished to leave; but the principal had locked the door, and put the key into his pocket. I glanced at the window, hoping to find a means of egress in that direction, though it was at least ten feet above the ground. But ten feet are nothing to a boy of spirit; and I was moving towards the window, intending to take the leap, when Mr. Parasyte sprang to his feet, and confronted me again. If ever a man wore the expression of a demon, the principal of the Parkville Liberal Institute did at that moment; and it was patent to me that, unless I could effect my escape, my trials and troubles had but just commenced.

I was more disposed to use strategy than force; for, in spite of the victory I had won, I was fearful that the tyrant "carried too many guns" for me. The malignity of his aspect was accompanied by an expression of pain, as though he had been injured by his fall. This was in my favor, if I was to be again compelled to break a lance with him.

"You villain!" gasped Mr. Parasyte, with one hand upon his side. "How dare you resist?"

"I have no fancy for being cut to pieces with a cowhide," I replied, as coolly as I could, which, however, was not saying much.

"Your uncle wished me to reduce you to subjection, and to flog you till you came to your senses."

"I am not very grateful to my uncle for his re-

9 *

quest; and I have to say, that I will not be tamely flogged either by you or by him."

"What do you mean to do?" demanded he, apparently astonished to find me so resolute.

"I mean to resist as long as I am flogged," I replied, twisting the cowhide I still held in my hand.

Saying this, I jumped upon the window-seat, and unfastened the sash.

"Stop!" said he, moving towards me.

"I know what you mean now; and if you come near me, I will hit you over the head with the butt-end of this cowhide," I replied, raising the sash.

"I intend to reduce you to subjection at any hazard," he added.

Without making reply, I attempted to get out of the window in such a way that I could drop to the ground, or "hang off" with my hands. In doing this, I laid myself open to the assault of the enemy, who was prompt in perceiving his advantage, and in availing himself of it. Seizing me by the collar with both hands, he dragged me back into the office, and hurled me heavily upon the floor, at the same time wrenching the cowhide from my grasp. I sprang to my feet with the celerity of a wounded tiger; but the principal began to beat me with a zeal corresponding to his malignity.

A heavy round ruler on the desk, which had before attracted my attention, was available as a weapon, and in the fury of my passion I grasped it. Without thought or consideration except in my own defence, I sprang upon the tyrant again, and dealt him several heavy blows with the implement, until one was planted in such a place on his head that it knocked him insensible upon the floor. Panting like a hunted deer from the rage which filled my soul, and from the violence of my exertions, I gazed upon the work I had done. Mr. Parasyte lay motionless upon the floor. I took the key from his vest pocket, and unlocked the door.

In the hall I found several persons, including Mrs. Parasyte, and Mr. Hardy, one of the assistant teachers. They had been sitting in the parlor opposite the office, and had heard the noise of the desperate struggle between the principal and myself.

"What have you done!" exclaimed Mrs. Parasyte, greatly alarmed when she saw her husband lying senseless upon the floor.

"This is bad business," added Mr. Hardy, as he hastened to the assistance of the principal.

"Is he dead?" asked the wife, in tremulous tones.

"No—O, no! But he has had a heavy blow on the temple," replied the teacher.

I assisted Mrs. Parasyte and Mr. Hardy in carrying my foe to his chamber. I was alarmed myself. I feared that I had done more than I intended to do. I went for the doctor at the lady's request; but before my return Mr. Parasyte had come to his senses, and complained of a severe sickness at his stomach. The physician carefully examined him, and declared that his patient was not seriously injured. I need not say that I was greatly relieved by this opinion. I left the room, intending to depart from the house, though it was now nearly eleven o'clock at night. Mr. Hardy followed me out into the hall, and wished to know where I was going.

"Home," I replied.

"I'm afraid you have got into difficulty, Thornton," added he.

"I can't help it if I have. I didn't mean to hurt him so badly; but it was his own fault."

"How did it happen?"

I told him how it happened; but Mr. Hardy expressed no opinion on the merits of the case. He knew, as well as I did, that Mr. Parasyte had been wrong from the beginning; but being in a subordinate position, it was not proper for him to condemn his principal.

"The boys are in a riotous condition, and it is fortunate they do not know of this affair. I hope you do not intend to inform them — at least not to-night," he added.

"No, sir, I do not. I have tried from the first to keep the peace. Poodles confessed to Mr. Parasyte that he had lied about the affair on the pier, but he refused to believe him. I am sorry there has been any trouble; but I couldn't help it."

Mr. Hardy was really troubled; but he could not say anything, and he did not. He was a poor man, trying to earn the means to study a profession by teaching, and a word or a look of sympathy to a rebel like me would have cost him his situation. He was a just and a fair man, and as such was loved and respected by all the students. Many of the boys

had often wished that he might be the principal of
the academy, instead of Mr. Parasyte, who had established and who still owned the institution.

There was nothing more to be said or done, and I
left the academy for home. I was sincerely sorry for
what had happened. Even a quarrel in which I
had been the victor had no pleasant reflections for
me. I would have submitted to any punishment
except the flogging, and borne the injustice of it
without a complaint; but I had been required to
confess that of which I was not guilty, and I
could not do that. I hated a lie of any kind,
and I could not tell one to save myself from the
consequences of the tyrant's rage and injustice.

I considered all the events of the day as I
walked home, and came to the conclusion that I
was not to blame for the mischief that had been
done. If I had been haughty and disobedient, it
was because I had been treated badly. I certainly
did not deserve flogging, and it would have been
impossible for me to submit to it. If I had been
guilty, I could have borne even that.

My uncle had counselled Mr. Parasyte to reduce

me to subjection; and much I marvelled that he had found words to say so much. It was an evidence of interest in me which he had never before manifested. It was plain that, in the settlement of the difficulty, I must count upon the opposition of my uncle, who had already espoused the principal's side of the quarrel. But I did not make any rash resolves, preferring to act as my sense of right and justice should dictate when the time for action came.

As I approached the cottage by the lake, I saw a light in my uncle's library. My guardian sat up late at night, and rose early in the morning. He did not sleep well, and he always looked pale and haggard. He was a misanthrope in the worst sense of the word. He seemed to have no friends, and to care for no one in the world — not even for himself. Certainly he had no regard for me.

Of his past history I knew nothing; but I had already concluded that he had been subjected to some terrible disappointment or injustice. He appeared to suffer all the time; and if he would have permitted it, how gladly would I have as-

suaged his woe by my sympathy! He was cold
and forbidding, and would not permit me to speak
a word to him. I had once tried to make him
tell me something about my father and mother;
but, with an expression of angry impatience upon
his face, he had turned and fled in disgust from me.

I longed to know who and what my mother
was; but my questions brought no answer. One
day, when my uncle was away, I had crept into
his library, and tried vainly to obtain some information from his books and papers. He caught me
in the room, and drove me out with a curse upon
his lips. After that a spring lock was put upon
the door, the key of which he carried in his
pocket.

On the present occasion I had nothing to expect
from my uncle; but I wished to see him, and tell
him my story. I knew that he could talk; for, during the preceding year, a man of thirty, elegantly
dressed, came to the cottage one afternoon, and
walked with my uncle into the grove by the lake.
They had business together, and it was not of a

pleasant nature; for, prompted by curiosity, I rowed my skiff up to the shore, to learn what I might of the stranger's purpose. I could not understand a word that was said; but my uncle talked rapidly and fiercely, and a violent altercation ensued, which I feared would end in blows. The stranger did not come back to the cottage, and the supper which Betsey had prepared for the guest was not needed.

Learning from this that my uncle had a tongue, I asked him who the stranger was. The answer was only a savage frown. He had no tongue for me. Neither old Jerry nor his wife was any better informed than I was, for both assured me they did not know the stranger. Satisfied, therefore, that my uncle could talk, I was determined to see him before I went to bed, though it was nearly midnight. Perhaps, also, I was disposed to adopt this course, because my guardian had given such bad advice to Mr. Parasyte. I was not insensible to the indulgence with which I had ever been treated; and seeing that my silent uncle wished to avoid me, I had generally favored him in doing so. It was different now. He

10

had given an order or a permission to have me brutally punished, and I was determined to make him "face the music."

I entered the house, and passing through my uncle's chamber, stood at the door of the library, which was fastened by the spring lock.

CHAPTER X.

IN WHICH ERNEST HAS AN INTERVIEW WITH HIS
UNCLE.

WITH my resolution still at the highest pitch
of firmness, I knocked at the library door.
I expected a storm; it was hardly possible to avoid
one; but I hoped, if I could induce my stern and
silent guardian to speak or to listen, that I might
make an impression upon him. There was no answer to my knock, and I repeated it. Then I
heard a stir in the library, and my uncle opened
the door. When he saw me, he was about to
close the door in my face, doubtless regarding my
conduct in knocking at his door as impudent in
the highest degree. I was not disposed to be shut
out, and anticipating his purpose, I stepped nimbly
into the room.

"Uncle Amos, I wish to speak with you for a few

moments, if you will be kind enough to hear me," I began, in tones as humble as the veriest tyrant could have required.

He sat down in his arm-chair, leaned his head upon his hand in such a way as to cover his face, but made me no reply, either by word or by sign.

"I would not trouble you if it were not necessary to do so," I continued. "Will you permit me to tell my story?"

He removed his hand, and gave me an affirmative nod; but it was evident to me that my presence was the occasion of positive suffering to him. I knew of no reason why I should be personally disagreeable to him, and it seemed to me that his aversion was caused wholly by a kind of obstinacy, which I could not understand.

"I have had a difficulty with Mr. Parasyte; but I was not to blame, as I can prove by more than half the students in the academy," I proceeded; and then I rehearsed all the particulars of my affray with Poodles, on the pier, including the rebellion of the students, and the confession of the guilty ones.

My uncle may have heard me, and he may not; but he took not the least notice of me, appearing to be absorbed in his own meditations during the recital of my wrongs.

"Mr. Parasyte called me into his private office, and informed me that he had been to see you," I added.

My uncle removed his hand from his face, glanced at me, nodded his head, which was the first indication he had given that he was conscious of my presence, after I began to relate my story. The look that accompanied the nod was anything but a pleasant one. There was something like malignant satisfaction in the glance that he bestowed upon me.

"Then you did request Mr. Parasyte to reduce me to subjection, as he expressed it?"

"I did," replied he, decidedly, as he again uncovered his face, and nodded to emphasize his reply.

This was hopeful, for I had at least got an answer out of him, though the reply was cold-blooded and cruel.

"Did you request him to flog me?" I demanded,

10 *

a little excited by the fact that my uncle was likely to prove as malignant as the schoolmaster.

"I did," he added; and his eyes seemed to glow like two coals of fire.

It was not difficult now for me to understand the situation. My uncle hated me, — why I knew not. I could not reconcile such a feeling with the indulgence he had always extended to me. I could not see why, if he hated me, as that fierce glare of his eyes indicated, he had always allowed me to have my own way, had always given me money without stint, and had permitted me to go and come when and as I pleased, and rove at will over the broad and dangerous lake.

I have since learned that this indulgence was perfectly consistent with hatred, and that the judicious parent, who truly loves his son, would deprive him of such unhealthy and dangerous indulgences. As he hated me, so he let me have my own way. Had he loved me, he would have restrained me; he would have inquired into my conduct when away from home; and above all, he would not have allowed me to risk my life upon the stormy lake as I did.

"You *did* request him to flog me, and without understanding the merits of the case!" I replied, indignantly.

He nodded again.

"Uncle Amos, I have tried to do my duty faithfully at school, and to be respectful and obedient to my teachers. This is the first time I have had any trouble. I say, most solemnly, I was not to blame."

"You were," said my uncle.

"Will you hear the evidence in my favor?"

"No."

"You will not?"

"No."

"What would you have me do?"

"Obey your teacher."

"Mr. Parasyte ordered me to apologize to Poodles."

"Do it then."

"But Poodles confesses that I was not to blame."

"No matter."

"I cannot do it, uncle."

"The master must make you do it," added my uncle, with a sneer.

"He attempted to do so. He began to flog me, and I knocked him down," I replied, quietly, but sullenly.

My uncle sprang to his feet, and stared at me with an intensity which would have made me quail if I had been guilty.

"You struck him!" exclaimed he, trembling with emotion.

"When he attempted a second time to flog me, I hit him on the head with a heavy ruler, and he fell insensible upon the floor."

My stern guardian rushed furiously across the room, foaming with passion.

"You villain!" gasped he, pausing before me. "You struck the master?"

"I knocked him down, as I would any other man who insulted me with a blow," I replied, firmly; for I intended to have my uncle understand exactly how I felt.

"You are an obstinate whelp!" ejaculated my guardian, who had certainly found a tongue now.

"All the students think I am right."

"The students! What do I care what they think?"

"They understand the case."

"Humph!" sneered my uncle.

"I see, sir, that I have nothing to expect from you," I continued.

"No!"

"I have only to say that Mr. Parasyte can't flog me. If I were guilty, I would not resist; but I will fight as long as I have a breath left against such injustice."

"Very pretty! May I ask what you are going to do with yourself?"

"I don't know yet; only, if I am not wanted here, I won't stay here. I think I can take care of myself."

"Do you consider this a proper return for all I have done for you?" asked he, more calmly.

"I don't know what you have done for me. I asked you once something about my father and mother, and you did not answer me."

"You have no father and mother," he replied, with visible emotion. "You need not ask any questions, for I will not answer them."

"Did they leave any property for me?" I asked,

mildly; and I had already concluded that they did, or my uncle would not have been so lavish of his money upon me.

"Property! What put that idea into your head?" demanded he; and he was more agitated than the circumstances seemed to warrant.

"I have no idea anything about it. I only asked the question."

"It is enough for you to know that I am willing to take care of you, and pay your expenses, however extravagant they may be, as long as you behave properly."

"I have always done so."

"No, you haven't! You have resisted your teacher, knocked him down, killed him for aught I know. You are a bad boy."

It seemed just as though my uncle intended to drive me to desperation, and compel me to commit some rash act. I could not see why he should refuse to tell me anything about my father and mother.

"I asked you whether my parents left any property for me. You did not answer me," I continued.

"I will answer no questions," replied he.

"If they did, it is right that I should know. it," I persisted.

"If they did, you will know it when you are of age to receive it."

"I would like to know whether you are supporting me out of your own property or with my own."

"It doesn't concern you to know, so long as you are supported."

"Yes, it does, and I insist upon knowing."

"I shall answer no questions," replied he, more troubled now than angry.

"If there is nothing belonging to me, I am very willing to go to work and support myself. I don't wish to be a burden upon one who cares so little for me as you do."

"I did not say you were a burden. I have given you all you asked for, and am willing to do so still."

"I don't wish to have you do so, if what you give me does not belong to me."

"You are a foolish boy!" said he, impatiently.

"You have hardly spoken to me before for a year; and you never said as much to me as you have to-night before in all my lifetime."

"It was not necessary to do so."

"Uncle Amos, I am old enough now to be able to think for myself," I continued, earnestly. "It is time for me to know who and what I am, and I am going to find out if it is possible for me to do so."

"It is not possible," said he, greatly agitated, though he struggled to be calm. "What do you wish to know?"

"About my parents."

He walked the room for a moment with compressed lips, as if considering whether he should tell me what I wanted to know.

"If I have concealed anything from you, it was for your own good," replied he, with a desperate effort. "Your father is dead; he died eleven years ago."

"And my mother?" I asked, eagerly.

"She is a raving maniac in an insane asylum."

This information came like a shock upon me, and I wept great tears of grief.

"I thank you, uncle Amos, for telling me so much, sad as it is. One more question and I am satisfied. Did my father leave any property?"

"No," said he.

I fancied that this single word cost him a mightier effort than all he had said before, though I could not see why it should.

"Where is my mother now?" I asked.

"You were to ask no more questions; and it is not best for you to know where she is," he answered. "Now, Ernest, I wish you to make your peace with Mr. Parasyte."

"How make my peace with him?"

"Do what he requires of you."

"I cannot do that; and I will not."

"If you persist you will ruin me," said my uncle, bitterly.

"I don't understand you, uncle Amos."

"Mr. Parasyte owes me a large sum of money."

Here was the hole in that millstone!

"His Institute is mortgaged to me. If there is trouble there, the property will depreciate in value, and I shall be the loser."

My uncle seemed to be ashamed of himself for having said so much, and told me to go to bed. I retired from his presence with the feeling that I must sacrifice myself or my guardian.

11

CHAPTER XI.

IN WHICH ERNEST IS DISOWNED AND CAST OUT.

I WAS so nervous and excited after the stirring events of the day, that I could not sleep
when I went to bed, tired and almost exhausted
as I was. I had enough to think of, and that
night has always seemed to me like a new era
in my existence. My father was dead; and my
mother, somewhere in the wide world, was an oc-
cupant of an insane asylum. My uncle had told
me I had no property, which was equivalent to
informing me that I must soon begin to earn my
daily bread, unless he chose to support me.

I would not even then have objected to earning
my own living; indeed, there was something pleas-
urable and exciting in the idea of depending upon
myself for my food and raiment; but I was not
satisfied with my uncle's statements. I could see

no reason why he should not tell me where my father had lived and died, and where my mother was confined as a lunatic. I meant to know all about these things in due time, for it was my right to know.

I could not help weeping when I thought of my mother, with her darkened mind, shut out from the world and from me. What a joy she would have been to me! What a comfort I might have been to her! My father was dead, and she had no one to care for her. Was she in a proper place? Was she kindly treated while overshadowed by her terrible infirmity? I shuddered when I thought of her, for fear that she might be in the hands of cruel persons.

It seemed very strange to me that my uncle should spend money so freely upon me if I had no expectations. Why should he wish to conceal anything that related to my father and mother from me? Who was the person that came to the cottage and quarrelled with him? I had reached the years of discretion, and was able to think for myself. What my uncle told me, and what he

refused to tell me, taken in connection with his conduct, his mode of life, and his misanthropic habits,
convinced me that there was something wrong. I
intended to ascertain what it was; and I was fully
resolved, whether it was right or wrong, to explore
the library in search of any letters, legal documents,
or other papers which would throw some light on
the mystery, now becoming painfully oppressive to
me. It was my duty, as a son, to assure myself
that my mother, in her helplessness, was kindly
cared for.

I went to sleep at last; and I did not wake the
next morning till nine o'clock, which was my uncle's
usual breakfast hour. I took my morning meal with
him; but he did not speak a single word. After
breakfast I went down to the boat-house. I missed
the Splash very much indeed; for I wanted to take
her, and sail away to some remote part of the lake,
and consider what I should do. Then it occurred to
me that my sail-boat might be raised and repaired;
and I was getting into the row-boat, with the intention of pulling out and finding the place where
the Splash had gone down, when my uncle made
his appearance.

"Ernest, have you considered what you mean to do?" said he. "Do you intend to go to school?"

"No, sir, I do not," I replied, promptly and decidedly.

"Then I disown you, and cast you out," he added, turning on his heel and walking back to the house.

Was I becoming obstinate and self-willed? Was I refusing a reasonable service? I sat down in the boat to think over it. It was not right that I should apologize to Poodles, after he had confessed that the evidence on which I had been condemned was a lie; and it was of no use for me to return to the academy unless I could do so.

Mr. Parasyte owed my uncle a large sum of money, secured by the estate and good-will of the Institute. If I was driven from the school, a majority of the boys would petition their parents to be taken from it also, and the establishment would be seriously injured. There was plainly an understanding between Mr. Parasyte and my uncle, or the tyrant would not have made war upon me as he did. Should I sacrifice myself in order to save my uncle's

11 *

money, or to prevent the debt from being im-
perilled?

No! I could not; but I hoped my uncle would
not lose his money, though it would not be my fault
if he did. I had just been " disowned and cast out."
The sentence hardly produced an impression upon
me. I was not banished from a happy home, where
I had been folded in a mother's love, and had lived
in the light of a father's smile; only from the home
of coldness and silence; only from shelter and food,
which I could easily find elsewhere.

I took the oars and pulled towards the bluff off
which the Splash had sunk. It seemed to me just
then that I was breaking away from all my early
associations, from my home and my school, and
pushing out on the great ocean of life, as my
boat was upon the lake. I must go out into
the world, and make for myself a name and a fortune. There was something solemn and impressive
in the thought, and I rested upon my oars to follow
out the idea. Breaking away! To me it was not
going away, it was *breaking* away. There was no
near and dear friend to bid me God speed on my

journey of life. As for my uncle, he would not
have cared if I had, at that moment, been forever buried beneath the deep waters of the lake.

I was awed and solemnized by the thought that I
was alone in the world. And looking up to the clear
blue sky, I prayed that God would help me to keep
in the path of truth and duty. I really hoped that,
if I had done wrong, or was then doing wrong, I
might be convicted of my error. I prayed for
light. I was afraid that I had been wilful and
wayward; but as I knew that I was right so far
as Poodles was concerned, I could not accuse myself of obstinacy in refusing to apologize. On the
whole, I was satisfied with myself, though willing
to acknowledge that in some things I had rather
overdone the matter.

Resuming the oars, I pulled towards the bluff. My
course lay near the shore until I had passed the north-
erly point of Parkville, where the steamboat wharf
extends a hundred feet out to the deep water of the
lake. Continuing beyond this long pier, I came in
sight of the Parkville Liberal Institute. As it was
then the middle of the forenoon, I did not expect

to see any of the students; but, to my surprise, I
discovered large numbers of them on the grounds
between the buildings and the lake. They did not
seem to be engaged in the usual sports, but were
gathered in groups on various parts of the premises.
Everything looked as though some important event
had transpired, which the boys were busily engaged
in discussing.

I was tempted to pull up towards the Institute,
and ascertain what had occurred, and why the students were not in the school-room, attending to their
studies; but I was fearful that my presence might
do mischief, and I reluctantly continued on my
way to the bluff. As nearly as I could interpret
the signs, the boys were in a state of rebellion,
though it was possible that Mr. Parasyte was too
ill to attend to his duties, and in the present excited state of the school, had deemed it best to
give the boys a holiday.

The bearings of the spot where the Splash sank
had been carefully noted, after my capture, by the
principal and his men, and without much difficulty I
found the place. The bed of this part of the lake

was composed of gravel, washed down by the con-
tinual wearing away of the bluff; and as the water
was clear, I could see the bottom. The Splash lay
in about twenty-five feet of water — as I found by
measuring with a fish-line. She sat nearly upright
on her keel, and the tops of her masts were not
more than a foot below the surface.

How could I coax her to the top of the water?
The Splash had been father and mother to me, and
I loved her. In my loneliness I wanted her com-
panionship. It did not look like an easy task to
raise her; and yet the most difficult things become
easy when we hit upon the right method of doing
them. The Splash was ballasted with ten fifty-sixes,
each with a ring for lifting it. They were deposited
on the bottom of the boat, where I could remove a
portion of them when I had a large party to take
out. I made up my mind, that with a long pole,
having a hook on the end of it, I could fasten to
the rings of the fifty-sixes, and raise them, one by
one, to the surface; and when the ballast was removed, the boat would rise of herself.

Satisfied that this idea was a practical one, I

started for Parkville to procure the pole. As I took the oars, I discovered that one of the Institute boats, which I had not before noticed, was pulling towards me. At first I was startled, fearful that it might contain some of my tyrant's minions, sent out to capture me, and carry me back to the school. As the boat came nearer, however, I saw that it was filled with my friends, prominent among whom were Bob Hale and Tom Rush; and I lay upon my oars to await her coming.

"Good morning, Ernest; I'm glad to see you," said Bob, as the Institute boat ranged up alongside of mine.

"What is the matter at the Institute? Don't school keep to-day?" I asked, when I had returned the salutations of my friend.

"There's big news there, Ernest, you'd better believe," replied Bob, in an excited tone.

"What is it? What has happened?"

"There has been an awful row between Mr. Parasyte and Mr. Hardy, and Mr. Hardy has been discharged — that's the first thing; and the fellows won't stand it, anyhow."

" What was it about? "

" We don't know. Mr. Hardy opened the school as usual at nine o'clock; but he didn't say a word to us about the troubles. A little after nine, Mr. Parasyte came in, with a black eye and a broken head. He and Mr. Hardy talked together a little while, and we saw that Parasyte was as mad as a hop. They went into the recitation-room to have it out; but in two or three minutes they returned, and Mr. Hardy said he was going to leave; but he didn't tell the reason — just bade us good by. If we had only known what the trouble was, we would have pitched Parasyte out of the window."

" Then Mr. Hardy has gone," I added.

" Left, and at once. Then Mr. Parasyte made a speech, in which he told us the school was in a state of rebellion; that Thornton had assaulted him, and struck him on the head with a heavy ruler, and that he intended to flog him till he apologized to Poodles, as his uncle wished him to do. We didn't wait to hear any more. We gave a yell, and rushed out of the school-room."

CHAPTER XII.

IN WHICH ERNEST RAISES THE SPLASH, AND THERE
IS A GENERAL BREAKING AWAY AMONG THE STU-
DENTS.

I LISTENED, with astonishment and dismay, to
the tale which Bob Hale told me. I could not
help asking myself to what extent I was responsible
for the troubles which overwhelmed the Parkville
Liberal Institute. I told Bob how I felt, and he
ridiculed the idea of my shouldering any portion
of the blame.

"Even the parson says you are not to blame, and
that you have behaved like a gentleman from the
beginning," said he, alluding to Henry Vallington,
who, on account of his intended profession, often
went by the name of the "parson."

"Can you imagine why Mr. Hardy was discharged?" I asked.

"We don't know; but it is easy enough to see that he blamed Mr. Parasyte, though he never said a word to the fellows. The idea of staying at the Institute after Mr. Hardy goes is not to be thought of," replied Bob, who, like myself, was a day scholar at the school. "What did Parasyte mean when he said your uncle wished him to flog you into subjection?"

"He meant that; my uncle told him to do so," I replied, with shame and mortification, not for myself, but for him who should have been my guardian and protector.

"Did he, though? Well, that was amiable of him," added Tom Rush. "He and Parasyte will do to go together."

"They do go together. I find that Mr. Parasyte owes my uncle a large sum of money. I had no idea that they were even acquainted with each other before," I continued.

"Then I wonder that Parasyte made a row with you, if he owed your uncle so much money."

"I don't understand it; but I think Mr. Parasyte didn't expect any trouble. He judged hastily be

12

tween Poodles and me, and when he had given his decision, he was too proud and too obstinate to alter it. I suppose he was a little afraid after what he had done, and went to see my uncle and ask for instructions."

"But it was cold-blooded for your uncle to say what he did."

"Probably Parasyte told his own story," I replied, willing to shield my uncle as much as possible.

"What did your uncle say to you when you went home?" asked Bob Hale, full of interest and sympathy.

"We had some words, and he disowned and cast me out — to use his own expression."

"Turned you out of house and home!" exclaimed Tom Rush.

"That was what he meant."

"Don't mind it, Ernest," interposed Bob. "You shall come to my house."

"I can take care of myself, I think," was my reply, rather proudly spoken.

"Of course you can; but you shall have half my bed and half my dinner as long as I have any."

"Thank you, Bob."

"We will talk that over another time, Ernest; for at present we have a big job on our hands."

"What is that?"

"We'll tell you by and by. Parasyte says you assaulted him, and hit him over the head with a big ruler. How was that, Ernest?"

I told them what had occurred after we left the school-room, and gave them all the particulars of my battle with the principal.

"Served him right," was the verdict of the boys. "He didn't tell us that he attempted to flog you; only that you pitched into him, apparently without any cause or reason," added Tom Rush.

"You all ran out of school," said I. "What is Mr. Parasyte going to do about it?"

"We don't know, and we don't care. He is a tyrant, and a toady; and all but about a dozen of the fellows are going to quit the school."

"But where are you going?" I asked, surprised at this decided step.

"We have it all arranged, and are going to break away in a bunch. We are getting things ready; but we want you, Ernest."

" Why me ? "

" Because you are a good sailor, and know all about boats ? "

That was highly complimentary in a direction where I was peculiarly weak — my love of boats and boating. Bob Hale then informed me that the students were going into camp on their own hook this year. This was an annual institution at the academy. Belonging to the Institute were seven tents, large enough to accommodate all the boys and all the teachers; and in the month of July the whole school camped out for one or two weeks. This custom did more for the popularity of the Institute than anything else, and without it, it was doubtful if the school could have been kept together; for it was an offset to the dislike with which a large majority of the boys regarded the principal.

The students had begun to talk about camping out as soon as the spring opened, and when the rebellion broke out, it immediately ran into this channel. The camp during the preceding year had been in a piece of woods ten miles east of Parkville; but the rebels had already decided to establish it, at the present time, on Cleaver Island, two miles north-west of the steamboat pier, and including an area of about twenty acres, well covered with wood.

I could not say that I approved of this scheme; but Bob Hale and Tom Rush said the students had unanimously agreed to it. I was not in favor of insubordination and rebellion. But the moral sense of the boys had been outraged; Mr. Parasyte had resorted to the grossest injustice, and they were determined to "break away" from him. Rather reluctantly I consented to join the insurrection. I ought not to have done so; but smarting as I then was under the injustice of my uncle and the principal, I found an argument to satisfy myself with my conduct.

The Splash seemed to be necessary, in my estimation, for the success of the enterprise, and my friends volunteered to assist me in raising her. I went to Parkville, and procured a long spruce pole, to which the blacksmith attached a hook. Without much difficulty the ballast was hoisted out of the sunken craft, and obedient to the law of gravitation, she came to the surface. We towed her to a bank of the lake

12 *

in the town, near the shop of a wheelwright, who
promised to have her repaired in a few hours. One
of the ribs was snapped off, and six of the "streaks"
stove in. We hauled her up on the shore, and got
the water out of her; and the wheelwright went to
work upon her at once, assisted by his journeyman.

I had regarded the Splash as a lost boat; and I
was delighted with my success in raising her, and
with the prospect of having her again as good as
new; for the wheelwright assured me she was not
materially injured in her timbers. The result of this
enterprise rather inflated my spirits, and not without
good reason; for, as I was now to take care of
myself, it had already occurred to me that I could
make money enough to support me by boating — for
there were always residents and strangers enough
in the town who wanted to sail to afford me a
good business for at least three months in the year.

"Now, Ernest," said Bob Hale, who had embarked
with me in my row-boat, "how shall we get the
crowd, the tents, and the provisions over to Cleaver
Island?"

"I don't think it is a very big job," I replied.

"I do. Of course Parasyte will prevent us from going if he can," said he.

"Too many cooks will spoil the broth," I added. "You want a leader, or captain, who shall manage the affair."

"We will choose you."

"No; I decline at the outset. I don't want the credit of being the ringleader in this scrape after what has happened."

"What do you say to the parson?" asked he.

"Capital!"

We consulted the students in the other boat, and they agreed to this selection. Both boats then pulled to the pier at the Institute. As we approached, all the rebels gathered around us. Bob Hale immediately called them to order, and made a brief statement of the necessity of the hour, and then nominated Henry Vallington as leader of the enterprise. He was unanimously elected, and somewhat to my surprise he accepted.

"Fellow-students," said the parson, in accepting the position, "if I didn't feel that every decent fellow in the Institute had been outraged and insulted by the conduct of the principal, I wouldn't have anything to do with such an affair as this. I want you all to understand that I, for one, am going into this thing for a purpose, and on principle."

"So say we all of us!" shouted the boys.

"Now, you must obey orders, and have no rioting or rows. We shall do this thing in order."

The boys were excited; but the parson told them to keep cool, and, when the orders came, to execute them promptly, which they promised with one voice to do. By this time I had a scheme arranged in my mind for the conveyance of the forces to Cleaver Island, and the leader did me the honor to appoint me master of transportation. I stated my plan to Vallington and two or three of the more influential of the boys. It was cordially approved.

At half past twelve the dinner bell of the Institute rang, as usual; and the boys, who had no idea of being deprived of their rations, marched in to dinner in order; and I went home with Bob Hale, who had invited me to dine with him. On our return, we learned that Mr. Parasyte had made a stirring appeal to the students, in the dining-room, to support the discipline of the school, and had intimated that he intended to prosecute Thornton in the courts for the assault upon him. I was rather startled at this intelligence, for a court was an appalling affair to me.

The boys heard in silence what the principal had to say, and left the dining-room in as good order as usual. At quarter before two the school-bell rang; but only about twenty obeyed the summons. I was on the pier at this time, and shortly after I saw Mr. Parasyte coming down to see the students. Deeming it best to keep out of his way, I pulled over to the wheelwright's, to look after the Splash. An hour later, Bob Hale, Henry Vallington, and Tom Rush joined me, saying that Mr. Parasyte had been very gentle with the boys, and had used only mild persuasions. Having failed in all, he had taken his horse and gone away. This was favorable to our operations, and I advised the parson to hasten back, and do the job at once.

At four o'clock the Splash was finished, and a

coat of paint put on the new streaks. I got under
way at once in her, taking my tender in tow. Near
the Institute lived a man who owned a large flat-
boat, or scow, used for bringing wood down the
lake. Tom Rush had hired this clumsy craft for a
week. The three row-boats belonging to the Institute had been manned by the boys, and were towing
this scow down to the pier, according to the plan I
had suggested to the parson. When the flat was
near the pier, a signal was given, and the boys on
shore all rushed to the building in which the tents
were stored. There were enough of them to carry
all the canvas, poles, and other materials at one
load, and the students rushed down to the pier
with them at a rapid pace, so that the work was
accomplished before any of the assistant teachers or
laborers could interfere.

The tents were tumbled into the scow, and all
the boys not needed in the row-boats embarked with
the camp material.

"All ready!" shouted Henry Vallington.

"Give way!" I added to the oarsmen.

OFF FOR THE ISLAND. — Page 143.

The long painter of the scow had been extended over, and fastened to, the three boats. As the wind was fresh, I went to the head of this line, attached a rope to the painter, and the procession of boats straightened out and moved off, dragging the scow after them.

CHAPTER XIII.

IN WHICH ERNEST IS CHOSEN COMMODORE OF THE FLEET.

THE procession of boats went off in good style, after the line was straightened; but the flat-boat was large and heavy, and it required a hard pull to put her in motion. The boys rowed well, and the wind was fresh enough to enable the Splash to do her full share of the work. The distance from the Institute to the island was two miles and a half, and at the rate we moved, I calculated that it would take nearly two hours to accomplish the voyage.

The movements of the students had been so sudden and so well arranged, that if any one saw them, there was not time to interfere before the boats were off. When the scow was fairly in motion, I saw Mr. Gaule, one of the teachers, and the two laborers on the estate, rushing down to the pier, apparently intent upon doing something.

"Come back, boys!" shouted Mr. Gaule.

No one made any reply, or took any notice of him.

"Come back, I say!" he cried again, but with no better result than before.

I was very glad that none of the boys made any insulting replies. They were as silent and dignified as so many judges. We all knew very well that Mr. Gaule had not force enough to attempt anything, and we did not expect to be molested until the return of Mr. Parasyte.

In something less than the two hours I had allowed for the passage, the procession of boats reached Cleaver Island. I was perfectly familiar with every foot of the shore, and I decided that the landing should be effected on the western side, at a point of land which extended out a short distance into the lake. The rowers landed and carried the painter of the scow on shore, by which they pulled the clumsy craft up to the bank.

The tents, cooking utensils, and other camp furniture, were landed and conveyed to the high ground in the southerly portion of the island. As soon as

this work was done, Henry Vallington intimated that
he wished all the boys to assemble near the point,
for a "powwow," to consult upon the state of affairs.
The word was passed from mouth to mouth, till all
the rebels had gathered at the appointed place.

"Now, fellows, we want to make arrangements
for doing this business in good order. When Mr.
Parasyte gets back to the Institute, and finds that
we are gone, he will not be likely to take it as
quietly as he has all day. Our breaking away has
really broken up the Parkville Liberal Institute,
and I shouldn't be surprised if its principal took
some decided steps. I haven't any idea what he
will do, but in my opinion he will do something."

"What can he do?" asked Tom Rush.

"He can do a great many things, and especially
a great many foolish things. I suppose, when we
come down to the niceties of the matter, we hadn't
any right to take the boats or the tents. In fact,
Mr. Parasyte stands *in loco parentis* to us."

"In what?" asked one of the boys who did not
study Latin.

"In the place of our parents; and therefore has

authority to do anything which parents might do. I can't help saying that I have no respect for Mr. Parasyte; that I despise him from the bottom of my heart. He knows, just as well as we do, that Bill Poodles made the trouble yesterday, and he persists in punishing Thornton for it. For such a man I can have no respect."

"So say we all!" shouted the boys.

"There is no safety for any of us, if we permit such injustice. He may take a miff at any of us any time. I hope that something good will come out of this scrape; and I think that something will."

I learned then, for the first time, that Vallington had drawn up a paper, setting forth the grievances of the students, in which several instances of Mr. Parasyte's injustice and partiality were related, and concluding with a full history of the affair between Poodles and myself. This paper had been signed by eighty-one of the students, and the publisher of the Parkville Standard had engaged to print it on a letter sheet, to be sent to the parents of the rebel scholars.

"Mr. Hardy has been discharged. He was the

best man in the Institute — just and fair. I don't know anything about it; but I am satisfied that he was sent away because he condemned Mr. Parasyte's treatment of Thornton."

"That was the reason," added Bob Hale. "Mr. Hardy saw Ernest last night, after the row in the office."

"I think we have the right of the case," continued Vallington, "though I suppose we are wrong in breaking away; but, for one, I won't see a fellow like Ernest Thornton browbeaten, and flogged, and ground down. If Mr. Parasyte wants to grind down one, he must grind down the whole."

"I am very much obliged to you," I interposed; "but I want you to understand that I don't ask any one to get himself into a scrape for me."

"When we protect you, Thornton, we protect ourselves. Your cause is our own. We won't say anything more about that matter. We are here now in a state of rebellion, and we must make the best of our situation. When Mr. Parasyte will give us fair play, we will return to the Institute."

"We will," replied some of the boys; but I am

free to say that they hoped he would not give them fair play until they had spent a week or more in camp.

"Now, fellows, we will see how we stand, and make arrangements for the future. We have boats and tents, and these are about all we have. We have provisions enough for supper and breakfast. We must get a supply of eatables to-night or in the morning. It will require money, but I suppose all of you have some; at any rate, I told you to bring your money with you, if you had any."

Most of the boys had some funds, which had been saved from their pocket money for a Fourth of July Celebration, planned months before.

"We need some officers, and as I don't believe in one-man power, I shall ask you to elect them. Please to nominate a treasurer."

"George Weston!" shouted one of the students.

"George Weston is nominated. All in favor of his election will manifest it by raising the right hand."

It was a unanimous vote, and the nominee was declared elected.

13 *

"Now we want to raise the money, we need to buy provisions, fairly. If any one will make a motion, it will be in order," added the chairman.

The Parkville Debating Society, an association connected with the Institute, had fully educated the students in parliamentary forms, and they were entirely "at home" in the business before them.

"I move you, Mr. Chairman, that each fellow be assessed fifty cents for expenses," said one of the students.

The motion was put and carried; and after Fred Mason had been elected clerk, the treasurer was instructed to collect the assessments forthwith. The next business was the selection of a commissary, and Tom Rush was chosen to this important office.

"Mr. Chairman, I nominate Ernest Thornton for commodore of our squadron," said Bob Hale; and, though the nomination created some merriment, on account of the high-sounding title of the officer, the vote was unanimous.

"I accept, Mr. Chairman; but I should prefer to be called simply the boatman," I replied.

"That won't do!" exclaimed Bob. "Ernest is to

have charge of all the boats, including the scow, and I am in favor of calling him commodore."

"We won't dispute about titles," laughed Vallington; "but the boats are all under Thornton's charge. I advise the commissary to consult with the commodore, immediately, in regard to procuring a supply of provisions for the company."

The rest of the business was soon completed. As an indication of the spirit of the boys, it was voted that the place should be called "Camp Fair Play." Vallington announced that six boys should be chosen each day to do the cooking and serve out the provision; that a watch should be kept around the camp night and day, to prevent a surprise from Mr. Parasyte and his forces; and that all work should be fairly divided among the students, with the exception of those who had been elected to offices. The boys then separated; and those who had been detailed to pitch the tents commenced their work.

"Commodore," said Tom Rush, laughing at the title.

"Mr. Commissary," I replied.

"Good! We are even, except that you are a bigger officer than I am."

"What can I do for you?"

"About the provisions — how shall we get them?"

"In the boats, of course," I replied.

"Do you think it will be quite safe for us to go back to Parkville?"

"We won't go there. It is only about six miles to Cannondale, on the other side of the lake. I think we had better go to-night, for we don't know what will happen to-morrow."

"That's a capital idea! I was thinking how awkward it would be to answer the questions that would be asked of us in Parkville. To-night it is. How many of us shall go?"

"Only you and I. The Splash will carry a good load. What are you going to buy?"

"We must live cheap," replied the commissary.

"I think we will bring off hams, potatoes, and bread or crackers."

"Those will be good feed. I advise you to make out a list of what you will want."

"I will do so."

"But we need not buy everything we want. The lake is full of fish, and I know just where to catch them."

"That's first rate," added Tom, with enthusiasm. "But it will take a heap of fish to feed all the fellows."

"I have caught a boat-load of lake bass and salmon trout in a day. I will agree to catch fish enough to feed the crowd for a week. But the fellows will want something besides fish to eat. Potatoes are cheap, and so are pork and bacon."

"When shall we start?"

"The sooner we go the better. We have no time to spare. There is a good wind now, and we may not have it much longer. I will land you at Cannondale in an hour; and if the breeze holds, we shall return by nine o'clock."

Tom Rush went to the treasurer to procure the funds he had collected, and hastened down to the Splash; but before the commissary joined me, a messenger came from Vallington to inform me that the lookouts on the bluff at the southerly end of the island had discovered a boat pulling towards the camp. I had a small spy-glass in one of the lockers of the Splash, with which I repaired to the bluff, to ascertain who the intended visitors could be.

"I suppose that boat bodes trouble to the camp," said the leader.

"I think it does, for it contains Mr. Parasyte and Deputy Sheriff Greene," I replied, after examining the boat through the glass.

CHAPTER XIV.

IN WHICH ERNEST IS WAITED UPON BY A DEPUTY SHERIFF.

WE had no means of knowing the object of Mr. Parasyte's visit to Camp Fair Play — whether he was coming to make a treaty of peace, or to declare and carry on the war. The boat in which he was approaching was a hired one, rowed by the two men who worked for him. His force was sufficient to do us a great deal of mischief; and the questions as to what he would, and what he could do, were full of interest to us. Four men are a formidable force to any number of boys; and the fact that Sheriff Greene was one of the party added to the seriousness of the visitation.

"What can they do?" asked Vallington. "We can at least prepare for possibilities."

"They can take the boats from us," answered

Bob Hale, "and leave us here to be starved into submission."

"It would be awkward to be obliged to return to the academy like whipped puppies; but I suppose we could be starved into it."

"We will look out for that," I added.

"How can you help it?"

"Leave that to me," I replied, as I hastened down to the landing-place, where I summoned my boatmen for service.

We took the three row-boats out of the water, and carried them some distance from the shore, hiding them in the bushes. The Splash was too large to be carried far; but we took her out of the water, and put her high and dry on the island. A force of twenty students had been placed under my command, and with a little engineering we made easy work even of these heavy jobs. The rudder of the sail-boat was unshipped, and concealed, so that she would be useless to the invaders, if they attempted to carry her off. There was no fear that they would try to tow the scow back to Parkville; for in doing this their punishment would be too severe.

Having accomplished my work, I returned to the headland where Vallington had his headquarters, just as Mr. Parasyte's boat touched the shore below.

"We are all right now," I remarked to the leader.

"The boats are secure — are they?"

"They are."

"Very well; then we are ready to receive our visitors. I will appoint a committee of three to wait upon them and invite them to our headquarters."

Three students were detailed for this duty, and they descended the bluff. Mr. Parasyte and the deputy sheriff followed them up the bank, where Vallington was ready to receive them in state, supported by his officers. The parson had instructed the rebels to treat our visitors with the utmost politeness, and enjoined them not to insult or annoy Mr. Parasyte. This was good advice, for some of the boys would have been glad to duck him in the lake, or to subject him to other indignities, now that they had the power to do so.

The principal of the Parkville Liberal Institute had doubtless been very angry when he returned

14

to the school, and found that a "breaking away" had taken place; but he had cooled off during his passage over the lake, and now he looked troubled and anxious, rather than angry. As he walked towards the spot where the officers of the camp stood, he gazed curiously around him; but he said nothing.

"Vallington, I am very much surprised to find you with this party," were the first words he spoke, as he discovered our leader, standing on his dignity, a little in advance of his supporters.

"Considering the circumstances, Mr. Parasyte, I am not at all surprised to find myself here," replied the parson. "If it were a mere frolic for the love of mischief, I should not be here. I presume you come on business, sir."

"On business!" exclaimed the principal, apparently taken aback by the remarks of Vallington. "I *did* come on business."

"You will oblige me by stating it, sir. I have been chosen the leader of this company, and I represent the students here assembled."

"My business is to order you back to the Institute," continued Mr. Parasyte, becoming a little excited by the independent manner of our leader.

"In behalf of those whom I represent, I must decline to obey the order — at least for the present."

The eye of the deputy sheriff twinkled as he listened to these speeches. He seemed to regard the affair as a big joke, and to appreciate it accordingly. Though none of us had ever had any official relations with him, we knew him as what all the people called "a good fellow," witty, jovial, and never severe even in the discharge of his duties. It is more than probable that he knew Mr. Parasyte as the boys knew him, and despised him accordingly. At any rate, we judged from the expression on his round face, that he was at heart on our side, however his official position might compel him to act.

"I am sorry, boys, that you have engaged in this rebellion, for it will not be pleasant for me to compel obedience," continued Mr. Parasyte, struggling to repress his anger.

"I am sorry, also, that we have been compelled to take this unpleasant stand," replied Vallington, with dignity. "If you are willing to hear it, sir, I should

like to state the position of the boys in this matter.
Perhaps the difficulty can be arranged; if it can,
we will at once return to the Institute."

"If there are any real abuses, I am willing to correct them. I will hear what you have to say."

Vallington briefly rehearsed the grievances of the
boys, and demanded that Thornton should be restored to all his privileges, without punishment, and
that Mr. Hardy should be reëngaged.

Mr. Parasyte turned red in the face, and bit his
lips with anger and vexation.

"Are you the principal of the Parkville Liberal
Institute, or am I?" said he, when the parson had
finished.

"Neither of us, I think, as the matter now
stands, sir."

"I see that you are determined to defy me," added Mr. Parasyte. "You ask me to restore Thornton
without punishment of any kind. Are you aware
that he assaulted me with a deadly weapon?"

"We are aware that he defended himself when
assaulted."

"Assaulted!" gasped Mr. Parasyte, astounded to

hear his own act called by such a name. "Are you aware of the powers which the law lodges in the hands of the teacher?"

"I am."

"Thornton refused to obey me; and, at his uncle's request, I intended to enforce obedience. It was my duty to do so."

"May I inquire, Mr. Parasyte, in what Thornton refused to obey you?" asked Vallington, in the gentlest of tones.

"I required him to apologize to Poodles privately, and to me publicly. He refused to do so."

"I told Mr. Parasyte that I would apologize to him," I interposed, addressing our leader.

"That wasn't enough," replied the principal.

"At the time, sir, you knew Poodles had confessed that he alone was to blame for the affair on the pier. Thornton was innocent; and it had been fairly proved to you that he was innocent. Poodles himself assured you of the fact, and his evidence was fully confirmed by Pearl. In the face of this overwhelming proof, you attempted to flog Thornton into apologizing for that of which you knew he was not

14 *

guilty. No boy with a soul would submit to be flogged under such circumstances. I would not. and I have no respect for any fellow that would. No boy was ever yet flogged in the Institute, and it was an outrage to attempt such a thing."

Vallington was quite eloquent, and Mr. Parasyte actually quailed as he poured out his feelings in well-chosen words, and with an emphasis which forced their meaning home to the heart. The tyrant had gone too far to recede. He did what weak, low-minded men always do under such circumstances — he got furiously angry, and delivered himself in abusive terms. He declared that Poodles and Pearl had been frightened into their confession, and persisted in saying that I had caused the quarrel on the pier.

"But it is no use to reason with you. I am going to compel obedience now. If you will not mind, I shall make you mind," foamed he, stamping the ground in his rage.

"We have nothing to say, sir, except that we shall defend ourselves from assaults of all kinds," added Vallington.

"Assaults! How dare you use that word to me! I am in the lawful exercise of my authority as the principal of the Parkville Liberal Institute. You were committed to my care by your parents, and I shall do my duty by you. As to Thornton, his case shall be settled by the court. Mr. Greene, you have a warrant for his arrest."

"Yes, I have," replied the deputy sheriff, with a broad grin.

"That's the boy," continued Mr. Parasyte, furiously, as he pointed to me.

My companions were evidently disconcerted, as I certainly was, by this action of Mr. Parasyte. They had got up the rebellion on my account directly, though indirectly on their own, and it would be a sad defeat to have me carried off by an officer of the law. Mr. Greene walked up to me, still wearing his smiling face.

"Well, Ernest, I am sorry for you; but I suppose I must do my duty. I have a warrant for your arrest."

"I shall not resist," I replied.

"You shall have fair play."

"That's all I want."

"I am sorry to take you away," he added, in a low tone; "for, between you and me, I think the boys have the rights of the matter; but I can't help serving the warrant."

"Put him in irons, Mr. Greene. He is a violent fellow," said Mr. Parasyte, savagely.

"I shall not do that," replied the sheriff. "I can handle him without any irons."

"Mr. Greene," interposed Vallington, "will you allow me to look at your warrant?"

"Certainly, if you want to."

"Don't do it, Mr. Greene!" shouted Mr. Parasyte.

"Don't be so grouty, sir. The young gentleman may see it, if he wants to do so," replied the sheriff, with a broad grin on his fat face, as he handed the warrant to the parson. "I don't belong to your school, Mr. Parasyte, and I suppose I can do as I please."

The principal bit his lip again; and Vallington glanced at the legal document.

"This warrant speaks about 'our county of Adicno,'" said the leader. "Are you aware, Mr. Greene, that this island is not in the county of Adieno?"

"No! Isn't it though?" laughed the sheriff.

"It certainly is not," added Vallington, returning the warrant to the sheriff.

"What odds does that make?" demanded Mr. Parasyte, angrily. "The offence was committed in Adieno county."

"Well, I don't know," said the sheriff. "I don't want to do anything that isn't lawful. It may be right to take him here; but I'm not sure, you see."

"That is absurd, Mr. Greene."

"I haven't been a deputy sheriff but about six months, and I'm not fully posted yet. We'll go back to Parkville, and if I find it's all right, I'll come over and arrest Ernest to-morrow. That will be soon enough."

Mr. Greene seemed to be the happiest person on the island; and Mr. Parasyte was so angry he could hardly contain himself.

CHAPTER XV.

IN WHICH ERNEST AND THE COMMISSARY VISIT CAN-NONDALE.

MR. PARASYTE, angry as he was, had sense enough left to see that he could accomplish nothing by remaining longer at Camp Fair Play. The spirit of freedom that prevailed there was unsuitable to his constitution.

"'I go, but I return,'" said he, in the language of Catiline to the Roman senate.

"When you return we shall receive you with all due respect, Mr. Parasyte," said Harry Vallington.

Mr. Greene chuckled, and shook his fat sides with suppressed mirth; and it was plain the principal had a very doubtful ally in the person of the deputy sheriff. And the ill-mated pair walked towards the landing, where we saw them embark, and leave the shore.

"Mr. Parasyte has more pluck than I gave him credit for," said Bob Hale, after we had silently watched the departure of the boat. "Isn't it a pity a man who knows so much, and is such a good teacher, should be a tyrant?"

"He is intellectually great and morally little," added the parson, with a savor of the cloth he was destined to wear. He has always been politic, and we have felt his tyranny only in little things, which are all the more mean because they are small. He is now fully roused; he is too obstinate to back out, even when he knows and feels that he is in the wrong; and now he will lay policy aside. I tell you, fellows, you must make up your minds for a hard battle, for Mr. Parasyte is in earnest. He will leave no stone unturned to reduce us to subjection; and if I mistake not, 'breaking away' will prove to be no joke. If any of the students feel like giving up, now is the best time to take the back track, for the farther we go the deeper in the mire we shall be. If there are any who are sick of their bargain, they had better say so now."

"No!" "No!" "No!" shouted the boys, till the sound became a unanimous voice.

"I see you are all of **one mind,**" continued Vallington. "I deem it right to tell **you** now **that, in my opinion,** Mr. **Parasyte is** no contemptible foe **to deal with.** He will **make a good deal** of trouble, if he does not **cause much anxiety,** perhaps suffering, in our ranks."

"What can he do?" asked one of the boys.

"I don't know. **He** hasn't told me what **he** intends to do, and probably **he will not,**" replied our chief, facetiously.

"Can't you guess?" asked another boy; and there seemed to be a general **desire to** anticipate the terrible things the principal **would** attempt **in order to** reduce the rebellious pupils **to** subjection.

"I am **no Yankee, and I** can't guess. I can mention several things he might **do.**"

"Tell us, **if** you please!" called **out one of the** more timid **of** the boys.

"**Very** likely he will attempt to **starve us** out by surrounding the island with boats, and preventing us from obtaining provisions. He must know that we have a very small stock **of** eatables on hand."

"We will trust to **our** commodore to break his lines, if he blockades **our** camp," laughed Tom Rush.

"He may come with a force of men in the night, and take away the boats."

"You said we should keep a watch at night," suggested **Fred** Mason.

"We hope the commodore will be able to protect his squadron," said Bob Hale.

"I shall do my best to insure the safety of the boats, or to run the blockade, if one is established," I replied, with becoming modesty; and in fact I was getting so excited over the prospect, that I rather hoped there would be an attempt to blockade us, or to carry off the boats, that I might have an opportunity to exercise my talent for navigation and strategy.

"And Mr. Parasyte may collect a force, and come over to capture the whole of us. He can charge us with stealing his boats, or something of that sort. He has already obtained a warrant for the arrest of Thornton, and to have him taken away from us would be about the worst thing that could happen," said Vallington.

"We will not let them take him," interposed a belligerent student.

15

" What will you do ? "

" Pitch the sheriff overboard," replied the spunky speaker.

" That will not do," I added. " I hope no fellow will think of such a thing as resisting an officer of the law."

" No, that wouldn't do," continued Vallington. " If Mr. Greene could not arrest Thornton because he was out of his county, Mr. Parasyte will get a sheriff from the proper county to do the job."

" That's so," said Bob Hale. " He will do his worst, you may depend upon that."

" I have an idea!" I shouted, under the inspiration of my new thought; and it really seemed to me like a brilliant suggestion.

" What is it ? " demanded our leader.

" Suppose we change our quarters ? "

" Where shall we go ? "

" To Pine Island. It is about seven miles from here, or nine miles and a half from Parkville," I answered.

" What shall we gain by moving ? " asked Vallington, deeply interested in my proposition.

"Several things. We are now six miles from Cannondale, where we must procure our provisions, while Pine Island is less than three."

"That's a decided advantage, if we are to be starved out," added the commissary.

"It is so far from Parkville that our movements could not be observed from the shore," I continued. "And Pine Island is at least four times as large as Cleaver Island, which would make it four times as difficult to blockade."

"Pine Island! Pine Island!" shouted the rebels, in concert, as they began to perceive the advantages of the proposed location.

"If the fellows don't object to working a part or the whole of the night, we might be in our new quarters before morning; and if we keep a good lookout, we may stay there two or three days before Mr. Parasyte finds out where we are."

"Pine Island! Pine Island!" was the chorus which came from the throng of boys, all of whom had gathered near the bluff.

"Those in favor of moving to-night, say ay," continued Vallington.

"Ay!" shouted the students, with one voice. "Those opposed, say no."

There was not a dissenting voice.

"It is a unanimous vote," added the leader. "Commodore Thornton, you are charged with the execution of this order, and you will make your preparations accordingly."

"But what shall we do for provisions?" asked the commissary, troubled about the proper administration of the affairs of his department. "We must have something to eat before dinner-time to-morrow; and if we are to keep out of sight, I don't see how we are to get anything."

"Perhaps Commodore Thornton can afford us some information on that subject," said Vallington. "Our safety and success depend mainly upon the vulgar things which the stomach requires."

"There is a good breeze now, General Vallington, and — "

The students interrupted me with a hearty laugh at the new title I had given to the parson.

"A truce to titles," laughed our leader.

"You call me commodore, and I think it is no

more than fair that I should give you your proper title."

"But you were duly elected commodore of our squadron."

"Mr. Chairman, I move that Henry Vallington be created general-in-chief of all our forces, by sea and by land," I continued.

"Second the motion," added Bob Hale. "I call upon the secretary to put the question."

The question was put by Fred Mason, and carried, unanimously.

"I am very much obliged to you for the honor you have conferred upon me; but we can hardly afford the time now to talk about titles. You were going to say something about the breeze, Commodore Thornton."

"I say that there is a good breeze now, General Vallington; and I think, if the commissary is ready, we can reach Cannondale in the Splash by nine o'clock. It is half past seven now," I replied, looking at my watch.

"The commissary is all ready," said Tom Rush.

"What time shall you return?" asked the general.

15 *

"By eleven or twelve. I think the fellows had better turn in, and sleep till we return," I suggested. "There will be time enough then to load the scow, and reach the island by daylight."

The general approved of this idea, but was afraid the boys were too much excited to sleep. I called those who had been detailed to serve as boatmen to assist in putting the Splash into the water, and, with Tom Rush alone, started for Cannondale. The breeze was fresh, and before the time I had mentioned we landed at our destination.

Since I had owned the Splash, I had spent all my vacations and holidays, and indeed all my spare time every week day when boating was practicable, on the lake. A spirit of adventure had prompted me to make long trips, and I had sometimes spent half the night in my lonely cruises. The darkness, therefore, was not an obstacle with me to the navigation of those familiar waters. I knew every point, headland, bay, and inlet, at midnight as well as noonday."

Lake Adieno, though a fresh-water lake, was not always the smoothest of navigation. Its shores were nearly level land, and there was nothing to shelter it from the blasts when the wind blew; and, with an uninterrupted reach of twenty miles from east to west, old Boreas had room enough to kick up quite a heavy sea. In a strong north-west or south-west wind, boating on the lake was no child's play.

We landed at Cannondale, and secured the Splash at the steamboat pier. For several years I had purchased the groceries for the cottage of my uncle; and since I had owned the sail-boat, I had as often procured them at Cannondale as at Parkville, and I was nearly as familiar with the streets of the former as with those of the latter.

We found a grocer and a provision-dealer, of whom Tom Rush purchased the supplies we needed. Of the former the commissary purchased ten kegs of crackers, and a variety of small stores, and of the latter sixteen hams, twenty pounds of salt pork, and twelve bushels of potatoes. At the baker's we obtained all the soft bread on hand — about a hundred loaves. These articles amounted to more than the assessments levied on the members, but Tom and I made up the balance. The provision-dealer harnessed his horse and carted the stores down to the pier;

and, grateful for the patronage we had given him, and the cash paid him, he asked no troublesome questions; and we simply told him that the goods were for the school, which was then camping out.

The Splash was loaded to her utmost capacity, and we decided to land the stores at Pine Island before we returned to our companions.

CHAPTER XVI.

IN WHICH ERNEST CONVEYS THE STUDENTS TO PINE ISLAND.

WE landed the provisions at Pine Island, and being still favored with a fresh breeze, made a quick run over to Cleaver Island. It was bright moonlight now, and very pleasant sailing on the lake. As we approached the landing-place, I discovered a row-boat pulling round the point below. My first thought was, that Mr. Parasyte was paying a second visit to the camp, intent upon carrying out the threats he had uttered.

"Can you make her out, Ernest?" asked Tom.

"It is a boat full of men or boys — I don't know which," I replied. "We will run down to her, and see what she is."

"It may be Parasyte."

"Very likely it is," I added, heading the Splash towards the intruder.

"What shall we do if it is?"

"I don't know that we can do anything but keep an eye upon him. I have a great mind to serve him as he did me yesterday — run him down, and sink his boat; but I won't do it."

I decided, however, to give him a scare; and with all sail drawing well, the Splash going through the water at a rapid rate, I ran directly for the row-boat. When we came within a few feet of the intruders, the fate that stared them in the face was too much for their nerves. They sprang to their feet, and begged me not to run them down. It was a startling scene for them; but at that moment I put the helm up, and ran astern of the row-boat, just grazing her as we went by.

"Boat ahoy!" I shouted as I put the helm down, and the Splash came up into the wind on the other side of the row-boat.

"Don't run into us," said one of the boys in the boat, whose voice I recognized as that of Bill Poodles; and by this time I had found that Mr. Parasyte was not one of the party.

"Who are you?" demanded Tom Rush.

" It's me," replied Poodles.

" Who's *me?* "

It was a disgrace to the Parkville Liberal Institute that any member of the school should use such execrable grammar, and we were not quite willing to believe that the party were fellow-students, with the exception of Poodles, from whom nothing better in the shape of correct speech was to be expected.

" I'm Bill Poodles — don't you know me?"

" Bill Poodles!" exclaimed Tom, in disgust. " What do you want here?"

" We have come over to see you," said another in the boat, whose voice was that of Dick Pearl.

" Well, what do you want?"

" We want to join you," answered Pearl.

" I don't know that we want you. Have you any news from the shore?" added Tom.

" We can tell you all that has happened since you left. We ran away after supper to join you," said Pearl. " If you will let us in, we will do all we can to help you."

" I don't know; I will speak to the general, and if he is willing, you may join; but you can't go ashore till he gives you leave."

Pearl, who seemed to be the leading spirit of the recruits, promised to wait off the shore till Vallington had been informed of his request, and his answer returned. The Splash filled away, and we landed at the point where the scow lay. We found that our enterprising general had not been idle during our absence. The tents had been struck, and the materials put on board the flat-boat. Everything was ready for the departure to Pine Island.

The approach of the row-boat had been noticed by the vigilant sentinels on the bluff, and the whole company had watched our interview with the new comers. Tom Rush reported on the case to our general, and it was necessary to act upon the request of the party for admission to the camp. In this matter there was less unanimity than had before been manifested, and several of the students were opposed to granting the request. Bob Hale was the most earnest among them, and declared that Bill Poodles, Dick Pearl, and the rest of the party could not be trusted; they were mean fellows, and we should be better off without them than with them. They were the "creatures" of

Mr. Parasyte, and they would make trouble if we admitted them.

It would have been well for us if this advice had been heeded, as the sequel will show; but it was not. Some of our best declaimers urged that there was power in mere numbers; and the strength of an harmonious union was yielded to this idea. The vote was in favor of permitting the recruits to be received; but a very respectable minority voted against it. Bob cheerfully surrendered the point, and Poodles and his companions were invited to land. When they came on shore, Vallington questioned them in regard to their intentions. They all made fair promises, and assured the general they would be good and faithful subjects.

Tom Rush had reported on the provision question, and gladdened the hearts of all the fellows when he stated what bountiful supplies of ham, bread, potatoes, and coffee had been deposited on Pine Island for the use of the party.

"Now, we are all ready to move," said Vallington. "The boats are all loaded, and we submit the rest of the job to the skill of Commodore Thornton."

16

"Move!" exclaimed Dick Pearl, and in the bright moonlight I saw him glance anxiously at Poodles.

"We have decided to break up our camp here and move to Pine Island."

"Be you?" said Poodles.

"We *be*," answered Vallington.

"If we had known it, I don't know that we should have come," added Pearl.

"What possible difference can it make to you whether we camp at Pine Island or at Cleaver Island?"

"I don't know."

"It is too late to back out now; you have found out where we are going, and you must go with us, to help keep the secret," said our general, decidedly.

Pearl and Poodles looked at each other, and evidently wished to consult together; but there was no opportunity.

For my own part, I was not satisfied with their conduct, and I determined to keep a close watch upon them; for it seemed to me, from their appearance, that they intended to make mischief. I whispered my suspicions to Vallington, who thought it was well enough to keep an eye upon them; but he did not believe ten such fellows as they were would attempt to interfere with the plans of the company. I assured him Pearl was a smart fellow, and under his lead the party might make trouble.

As the wind was not only fresh, but fair for our passage to Pine Island, I rigged one of the tent poles as a mast for the flat-boat, intending to save the boys the hard labor of towing her seven miles. I secured another pole across the mast for a yard, to which I bent on the canvas of one of the tents for a sail. There was a heavy steering oar in the boat, which answered the purpose of a rudder. Having adjusted all this gear to my satisfaction, we pushed off, and I took my station at the helm of the flat-boat, which was crowded with boys.

I appointed Bob Hale, who had some experience as a boatman, to the charge of the Splash, though, as a matter of prudence, I directed him to set only the jib and mainsail. The row-boats were towed alongside the scow. The sail fully answered all my expectations, and the old "gundalow" actually made about three knots an hour under her new rig. The students stretched themselves on the tents, and very likely some of them went to sleep, for it was now two o'clock in the morning, and most of them were tired out, and gaped fearfully.

It was daylight when we ran into the little sheltered bay where we had landed the goods from the Splash. It was quite chilly in the morning air, and the fellows were glad of the exercise required to unload the scow and pitch the tents. But in a couple of hours the work was done, and the weary laborers were glad enough to stretch themselves on the beds of pine foliage in the tents. All the boats were hauled into an inlet, where they could not be seen by any passing craft on the lake, and I felt that everything was safe.

Everybody was worn out, and I think everybody went to sleep, even to the sentinels, who were stationed where they could give notice of the approach of any intruders. I was so exhausted myself that I should have slept if I had known all the deputy sheriffs in the state had been after me. And there we all lay till noon, buried in slumber. And when we awoke there appeared to be no life anywhere but on the island. The lake was calm and silent, and from the distant shores not a sound came to disturb us.

When the boys did wake they were wide awake, and immediately voted that "breaking away" was a capital idea. It was then unanimously resolved that it was time to have something to eat. The boys had had some experience in the culinary art in previous campaigns, and we had all the pots, kettles, and pans provided for such occasions. A fire was made in the woods, near the centre of the island, where it was hoped the smoke would not betray us, and potatoes and ham were soon hissing in the pans. About twenty of the students were employed in this work, — peeling potatoes, and preparing the pork and bacon, — while only four of the most experienced were intrusted with the care of the actual cooking. We had a big meal, though we had no knives and forks, or plates. The company was divided into messes of ten each, there being one large tin pan for each, from which the boys took the "grub" with sharp-

16*

ened sticks or jackknives. We enjoyed it quite as much as we did our dinners at the Institute.

We passed a quiet day, without interruption from within or without. We neither saw nor heard anything from Mr. Parasyte, and the Poodles party behaved better than we had expected, so that we had learned to trust them. The necessary work of the camp was all we could do, and when night came we were glad to turn in at an early hour, for we had not yet fully recovered from the fatigues of the previous day and night.

It was ordered by the general-in-chief that the watch during the night should be relieved every two hours, and that three should be on duty at once. A sufficient number of the company were detailed for this purpose, and a tent apart from the rest assigned to them, that others might not be disturbed when the watch was changed. How faithfully this watch performed their duty we learned from the developments of the next day.

I turned out about five o'clock in the morning, intending to try my hand at fishing with

Bob Hale and Tom Rush. We went down to the inlet where the squadron had been secured, to obtain one of the row-boats.

There was not a boat there!

Even the old scow had disappeared, and the Splash was nowhere to be seen!

CHAPTER XVII.

IN WHICH ERNEST FINDS THERE IS TREASON IN THE CAMP.

WHAT had become of the boats? I was a commodore without a squadron, and I felt so cheap that I would have sold out my commission for sixpence, and thrown myself in. The boats had been carefully secured, under my own direction, in the little inlet, and they could not have drifted away. I looked at Bob Hale, and Bob Hale looked at me; but neither of us could explain the disappearance of the fleet.

"An enemy hath done this," I began, in Scripture phrase.

"Of course it couldn't have been done by a friend," added Tom Rush. "It's lucky we have a good stock of provisions on hand."

"But the stock won't last forever," suggested Bob.

"We are not going to be starved out in a week, or a year, for that matter," I interposed. "We are not to be broken up by any such accident as this."

"The commodore is spunky," laughed Bob, who was always good-natured, whatever happened.

"I am not to be put down by any such expedient as this taking away the boats. When I want to visit the main shore, I shall do so, boat or no boat," I replied; for I already saw how I could counteract the misfortune of the loss of our squadron.

"Parasyte has snuffed us out, I suppose, and sent a party up here in the night to take the boats," continued Bob Hale. "He means to starve us out."

"He will discover his mistake. But let us take a look round the island; perhaps we may find out what has become of the boats;" and I led the way to the nearest point, at which a sentinel had been stationed.

The student on watch there knew nothing of the absence of the boats. There had been no alarm given at the guard tent. We walked around the island without obtaining any information of the lost squadron. We reported the mishap to Vallington, who was both surprised and indignant.

The occupants of the guard tent were all turned out, and those who had been on watch during the night were examined; but none of them knew anything about the boats. They had not heard any noise during the night, or seen anything on the lake. The general then mustered the company, and after stating what had occurred, called for any information; but no one had any to give.

"Where is Bill Poodles?" suddenly demanded Bob Hale, as he glanced around among the students.

"He is not here," replied Tom Rush, after he had scrutinized all the faces.

"And Dick Pearl?"

"Not here."

"Is any of the party that came off that night present?" demanded the general.

"No," answered several, after each fellow had looked his neighbor full in the face.

"That's what's the matter!" exclaimed Bob Hale. "Bill Poodles and the rest of them have run away with the boats; and in my opinion that's what they joined us for."

A further examination convinced all present that this was the fact. It looked as though Mr. Parasyte had sent off the ten boys who joined us on the first night, to rob us of the boats. We remembered the dismay with which Pearl and Poodles had listened to the announcement of our intended removal from Cleaver Island, and were fully confirmed in our view of the traitors' purpose.

We found that the conspirators had all occupied the same tent, and one of the fellows who slept with them now remembered that he had half waked up, and heard Dick Pearl talking in a low tone to some one. Vallington called up the sentinels again, and spoke pretty sharply to them of their neglect of duty.

"It would have been impossible for them to carry off the boats if you had been awake; and now you have got us into a pretty scrape. We shall have to back out, and march back to the Institute like whipped puppies," said he, with becoming indignation.

But the sentinels protested that they had kept awake all the time.

"Tell that to a dead mule, and he would kick your brains out," replied the general. "Who stood at the south station?"

"I did from ten till twelve," answered Joe Slivers; "and I am sure no boat went out of the cove during that time."

"And who from twelve till two?" continued the general.

No one answered.

"Who was it—don't you know?" demanded Vallington, sternly.

"I know," replied Ben Lyons. "It was Carl Dorner, for I had the north station at the same time."

"Carl Dorner!" exclaimed Bob Hale. "He was one of the Poodles party."

"That accounts for it," added Vallington. "Who had the east station from twelve till two?"

"Mat Murray," replied Slivers.

"He's another of the Poodles tribe," added Bob. "It's as clear as mud now. We put traitors on guard, and we are sold out."

"Ben Lyons, you had the north station from twelve till two," continued the general.

"I did; but I was nearly half a mile from the cove," replied the sentinel.

"And Carl Dörner and Mat Murray had the east and south stations at the same time."

"They did."

"Who called the fellows that were to relieve you?"

"I did," answered Lyons.

"Didn't you miss Dorner and Murray?"

"I didn't notice them; but I did see the three fellows who went on guard at two o'clock. They started for their stations, and I turned in, without thinking anything about Dorner and Murray."

It further appeared that the two traitors had used some "shuffling" to obtain the east and south stations. It was evident now that the conspirators had executed their plan shortly after midnight, while their associates were on guard at the two posts where their operations could be seen or heard. The south station was on a point of land which commanded a full view of the cove where the boats lay. From the east station the lake in the direction of Parkville and Cannondale could be seen. From the north

17

station, which was considerably farther west than either of the other posts, nothing could be seen on the south side of the island.

If the conspirators had gone to the eastward with the boats, they could easily have kept out of sight of the sentinel at the north station — the only true one on duty when the mischief was done — by hugging the main south shore of the lake. If they had gone to the westward, or farther away from Parkville, — which was not likely, — they could not have been seen by Ben Lyons till they had gone at least a mile.

In the mud at the bottom of the cove we found a pole sticking up, which the traitors had probably used in pushing the scow out into the lake. This showed us in what manner they had gone to work; but I was satisfied that they had not attempted to tow the scow any distance; it would not have been possible for them to do so. It was comparatively easy to move her with setting-poles, but they could have done nothing with the unwieldy craft in the deep water. I therefore concluded that they had merely pushed her out into the lake, and then turned her adrift. It was probable that she had been driven ashore by the north-west wind somewhere in the vicinity of Cannondale.

What the conspirators had done with the Splash was not so clear to me, for not one of them knew anything about the management of a sail-boat. She had a pair of oars on board, and it was probable they had rowed her, as they had the other boats. All the sentinels agreed in their statements that the wind had blown pretty fresh in the night, and I was not quite willing to believe that the ten faithless ones had pulled the four boats the whole distance to Parkville, which was nine miles, in the heavy sea that must have been caused by a brisk north-west wind. They were not boatmen enough to undertake such a job, or to carry it through if they did attempt it.

Cannondale lay to the south-east of Pine Island, and with the prevailing wind of the night, it was an easy matter to accomplish the two miles which lay between them. After a great deal of thinking, reasoning, and studying, I came to the conclusion

that the Splash, and perhaps two or three of the
four row-boats, — for the conspirators had added
one to our original number, — were not farther off
than Cannondale. The wind was still fresh from the
north-west, and the traitors would hardly care to
pull even a single boat eight miles. The steamer, on
her way to Parkville, would touch at Cannondale
about one o'clock, and I surmised that the deserters would return in her.

I made up my mind, in view of these facts and
suppositions, that it would be advisable for some of
our party to visit Cannondale before one o'clock.
Pine Island had sometimes been used as a picnic
ground, and the people had been conveyed thither
in a steamer. Near the south station, in the deepest water, there was a rude pier of logs built out,
for the convenience of landing the parties. This
loose structure suggested to me the means of reach-
ing the main shore; and, without waiting for breakfast, I "piped" away my boatmen, and proceeded to
build a raft.

Placing three large logs in the water, we lashed
them together, and covered them with short pieces

of board, from the ruins of an old cook-house on the island. The job was finished when breakfast was ready, about seven o'clock, including a mast and sail, the latter made of the curtain of a tent. The preparations I had been making had a wonderful effect in warming up the spirits of the boys, considerably depressed by the prospective calamities which were supposed to lie in the wake of the loss of our boats; and at least three quarters of them applied to me for permission to join my expedition to the main shore. I determined, however, to take but four with me, among whom were Bob Hale and Tom Rush.

As soon as we had eaten a hearty breakfast, we embarked, and hoisted the sail on our clumsy craft. When she had passed out of the cove, she took the breeze, and went off at a very satisfactory pace towards Cannondale, plunging and rolling in the heavy sea like a ship in a gale. With us as navigators, "the die was cast," for it would be impossible to return to the island unless the wind changed, for the raft would only go before it.

The craft dived down and jumped up, and every

17*

wave swept completely over it; but we had taken off our shoes and stockings, and rolled up our trousers' legs, so that we suffered no inconvenience. The fresh breeze carried us over in about half an hour, and the raft was thrown high and dry on the beach, a quarter of a mile below the town.

CHAPTER XVIII.

IN WHICH ERNEST AND HIS COMPANIONS LAND AT CANNONDALE.

WE landed on the beach, put on our shoes and stockings, and walked towards the village of Cannondale. It was still early in the morning, — as people who lie abed till breakfast measure time, — and I was quite confident that I should find the boats, if not the deserters from our camp, at the town. The fact that none of the party were boatmen assured me they could not have gone on to Parkville. The wind must have brought them to Cannondale, and must have prevented them from leaving it.

We followed the beach from the point where we had landed until we came to the steamboat pier, which was the usual landing-place for all boats.

On the further side of the wharf, sheltered from

the wind and the sea, was our entire squadron, with the exception of the flat-boat.

"We are all right now," said Bob Hale; and we broke into a run, and hastened over to the point where the boats were secured.

"Where do you suppose the deserters are?" asked Tom Rush.

"Probably, as they didn't sleep any last night, they have gone to bed at the hotel," I replied. "It will be a good joke for them, when they wake up, to find they have had their labor for their pains."

On the steamboat wharf there was a building used for the storage of goods. Just as I was about to go down the steps at the foot of which the Splash lay, with the row-boats made fast to her, a lame man came out of the warehouse, and hailed us.

"What do you want?" he demanded, in no conciliatory tones.

"I want this boat," I replied.

"You can't have her," he added, decidedly.

"Why not?"

"Because you can't."

"That doesn't seem to be a very good reason," I

answered, descending the steps, and jumping into the Splash.

"Do you hear what I say?" demanded he, in savage tones.

"I do; I am not deaf, and you speak loud enough to be heard," I added, as I proceeded to remove the stops from the mainsail, preparatory to hoisting the sail.

"Are you going to mind what I say, or not?" he shouted, in loud tones.

"I am not."

"That boat's in my charge, and you can't have her."

"I don't care whose charge she is in. The boat belongs to me, and I intend to have her."

"Who are you?"

"It doesn't matter who I am; but I take it any one has a right to his own property, wherever he finds it."

"Can you prove that the boat is your property?" asked he, in a milder tone.

"I can, but I shall not take the trouble to do so," I replied, with more impudence than discretion.

"All I've got to say is, that you can't have that boat," added he, angrily; and he came down the steps, and took position by my side in the Splash.

"Come aboard, fellows!" I called to my companions.

"I suppose you claim these row-boats too — don't you?" said the lame man, with a sneer.

"I do not," I answered, concluding, under the circumstances, to go no farther than the facts would warrant. "Those boats belong to the Parkville Liberal Institute."

"I know they do," growled the man, who seemed to be in doubt what to do.

"Hoist the jib, Tom. If you wish to land, sir, now is your time," I suggested to the intruder, as I picked up the heavy oak tiller of the Splash.

"What are you going to do with that tiller?" continued he, fixing his eye fiercely upon me.

"I am going to steer the boat with it," I replied. "If you wish to go with us, I shall not object to your company."

I saw that the man only wished me to bully and

threaten him a little, to induce him to pitch into me, though it was plain he did not like the looks of the heavy tiller in my hand. I refrained from provoking him any further than to persist in claiming possession of my boat.

"You say this boat is yours," said he, after a moment of deliberation.

"I do; if you need any proof, I will now refer to Mr. Leman, the grocer, and Mr. Irwin, the provision-dealer; and if you belong on this wharf, you must have seen me land from her more than once."

"I don't want to quarrel with you," he added. "I know the boat very well, and very likely I've seen you in her; but I don't remember. I live close to the shore beyond the village, and I was waked up in the night — it was about one o'clock, I guess — by a lot of boys hollering. I got up, and found all these boats heaved up on the beach, and the boys trying to get 'em off. I helped 'em a while, and then brought the boats round here, for they would all got stove to pieces there."

The man talked very well now, and I met him in the same spirit.

"The boys who got into the scrape ought to pay you for helping them out," I replied.

"I don't like to be turned out of my bed in the night to do such a job for nothing."

"You must make them pay you."

"They said they would, or that the schoolmaster over to Parkville would, for he sent them to look out for some boys who had run away."

"Did they?" I replied, glancing significantly at Bob Hale, for this acknowledgment implied that Mr. Parasyte had sent the deserters to do the work they had accomplished. "But I don't see that we have anything to do with the matter. If I were you, I would hold the other boats till they paid me for my trouble."

"I'll do that."

"How much do they owe you?" asked Bob.

"Well, I don't know; they ought to give me a couple of dollars, I think," replied the man.

We passed a few words among ourselves, and Tom handed the man two dollars.

"That's to pay for saving this boat," said Tom. "We ought not to pay it, for our boat was stolen from us; but you must collect as much more before you let the other boats go."

"Thank ye," replied the man, with a broad grin, indicative of his satisfaction, as he took the money. "I spoke rather sharp to you at first, because I thought you were going to take the boats without paying for the job I did. I didn't mean nothing by it, and I hope you'll excuse it."

"It is all right."

"You can take the other boats too, if you like," continued the man, magnanimously.

We concluded that we did not want them. They were of no service to us, for with a south-west wind, I could work the scow over to Parkville; and I intended to go in search of her in the Splash.

"Did the fellows that came in these boats say anything to you about where they came from?" asked Bob Hale of the man.

"They told me all about it; but I knew something about it yesterday, for the schoolmaster came over here in the steamer, inquiring after you. He said you went to the Cleaver first, and then left — he didn't know where you was now."

18

"Mr. Parasyte here!" exclaimed Tom Rush.

"He's at the hotel, and he's going to find you and bring you back to-day," added the man, with a laugh. "You have done the handsome thing by me, and I don't mind telling you all about it."

We could scarcely believe that this was the man who had been so intent upon quarrelling with us; but it seemed he supposed we were the same boys who had come in the boats, and intended to cheat him out of his money for the job he had done.

"What is he going to do?" asked Bob Hale, rather excited.

"He has engaged the Adieno, and is going to look for you."

"The Adieno!" ejaculated Tom Rush.

The Adieno was a small steamer, owned in Parkville and Cannondale, employed in towing, conveying pleasure parties, and other uses on the lake. She was lying at the other side of the steamboat pier, and the smoke was already rolling out of her smokestack. Our informant did not precisely know in what manner Mr. Parasyte intended to proceed;

and we could not ascertain whether he intended to bring off our party by force, or to resort to some milder means to break up the camp; but we were very grateful for the information we had obtained. By this time Mr. Parasyte had learned from the deserters where we were.

Our new-made friend, who, I think, had learned to respect me for the decision with which I had answered him, went up the steps. As he did so, he repeated his offer to allow us to take the other boats, which we again declined.

" He's coming!" said our new ally, as he reached the cap-sill of the wharf.

" Who ? "

" The schoolmaster, and all them boys. Be in a hurry! He's close by."

I ran the mainsail up, and cast off the fasts which secured the Splash; but just as I had pushed off from the steps, Mr. Parasyte, attended by the deserters, appeared on the wharf. The eyes of the latter opened wide when they saw our party in the Splash, and it appeared to be a great mystery to them how we happened to be on the main shore, when they had left us on the island without a boat or craft of any kind. We were behind the wharf and building, so that the sails of the Splash did not get the wind, and I told a couple of my companions to take the oars.

"Stop, Thornton!" shouted Mr. Parasyte.

"Hold on a minute, and let us hear what he has to say," said Bob Hale.

We waited, looking up at the principal of the Parkville Liberal Institute to hear what he had to communicate. Mr. Parasyte went down the steps with the deserters, and they got into a couple of the row-boats.

"We are ready to hear anything you have to say," called Tom Rush.

"I simply wish to know whether you intend to compel me to use extreme measures," said Mr. Parasyte, as, by his direction, Dick Pearl pushed the boat in which they stood towards the Splash.

"We will return to the Institute when you comply with the terms stated by Henry Vallington," re-

plied Bob Hale, as the bow of the row-boat came up
to the stern of our craft.

"Perhaps I did not clearly understand what that
proposition was," said Mr. Parasyte, as he turned
and said something to Pearl which we could not
hear.

Bob was going to restate the terms, when Pearl
suddenly made fast the painter of his boat to a ring
in the stern of the Splash.

"Only to hold her for a moment," said the
principal, as he stepped into the bow of the row-
boat.

We watched him closely. The other row-boat,
in which six of the deserters had taken their
places, was also working up to the Splash. I
decided that we were getting into a scrape, and
told my companions with the oars to pull. They
obeyed, and in a moment we caught the stiff
breeze; the Splash forged ahead, twitching the row-
boat after it.

"Hold on tight, Pearl!" said Mr. Parasyte, savagely, now indicating that he meant war, and not
peace.

18*

I dragged the boat half a mile from the shore, and then, in tacking, gave it such a sudden twitch as to throw Mr. Parasyte, who was still standing, off his balance, and he went over the side into the angry waters.

CHAPTER XIX.

IN WHICH ERNEST AND HIS FRIENDS ARE DISGUSTED WITH MR. PARASYTE'S INGRATITUDE.

IT was very imprudent in Mr. Parasyte to stand up in a boat, while being dragged through the water at such a rapid rate as the Splash was going. I tried my best, before the accident, to detach the painter of his boat; but Pearl had passed the rope through the ring, hauled it back, and made it fast on the stem of his own craft. It was my intention to cut it as soon as I came about, and I had taken out my knife for the purpose.

When the Splash tacked, the row-boat ran up to her stern, slacking the painter. As this was a favorable moment for Mr. Parasyte, who was determined to "board" us, he was on the point of stepping forward. As soon as the sails of our craft caught the breeze, she darted off again, straightening the painter, and giving the principal's boat such a fierce jerk, that it not only upset Mr. Parasyte, but heeled his boat over so that she half filled with water.

"Help! Help!" shouted Mr. Parasyte, in tones which convinced us that he fully appreciated the perils of his position.

"Let go your painter, Dick Pearl!" I shouted.

"I can't; we are half full of water," replied he.

It was useless to argue the point, and with the knife I had open in my hand, I severed the half-inch rope, and permitted the row-boat to go adrift. There was a heavy sea for an inland lake, and the row-boat made very bad weather of it, in her water-logged condition.

"Don't leave us, Thornton," said Dick, with what self-command he had, while Bill Poodles, who was with him, actually blubbered with terror.

"Sit down and bale out your boat!" I called to them, as I put the Splash about to save Mr. Parasyte. "Keep cool and you are all right. Bale out your boat!"

"We have no dipper."

When my boat had come about, I ran her close

to them, and tossed a small bucket to Pearl, with which he went to work to free his boat from water. The circumstances were by no means desperate, though Pearl was the only fellow among them who appeared to have any self-possession.

"Help! Help!" shouted Mr. Parasyte, more feebly than before.

"Go forward, Bob, with the boat-hook; and stand by, Tom, to help him. Let him get hold of the boat-hook."

I swept round in the Splash, till I threw her up into the wind with Mr. Parasyte under the bow. Bob Hale extended the boat-hook to him, which he promptly grasped, and with some difficulty we hauled him on board. It was a warm day in June, and I did not think him any the worse for the bath he had taken; but I was perfectly satisfied that he would have been drowned if we had left him to be rescued by Pearl and his party. We felt that we had done a good thing — that we had rendered good for evil.

For my own part, judging by what I should have felt in his situation, I expected some conciliatory proposition from him; and we waited, with no little interest and anxiety, till he had wiped his face and neck, and adjusted his damp linen as well as he could. He had the satisfaction of knowing that I, the rebel, who had resisted him, and whom he regarded as the author of all the mischief, had saved his life; and I am sure that it was a greater satisfaction to me than it was to him. I ran the Splash up towards the deserters, who were still employed in baling out their boat.

Mr. Parasyte spoke at last. Though I knew he was a tyrant, though I knew there was nothing that could be called noble in his nature, I did not expect what followed. I supposed there was some impressible spot in his heart which might have been reached through the act we had just done.

"So you meant to drown me — did you?" were the first words he said, and in a tone so uncompromising that we saw at once there was nothing to hope.

I looked at Bob Hale, and Bob looked at me. Our surprise was mutual; and as there was nothing that could be said, we said nothing.

"You meant to drown me — did you?" repeated Mr. Parasyte, with more emphasis than before.

Bob and I looked at each other again. Grave as was the charge he indirectly preferred against us, there was something so ludicrous in the making of it by one whom we had just pulled out of the water, that I could not help smiling. Mr. Parasyte saw that smile, and as he always put the worst construction upon what was done by those not in favor, he misinterpreted it, and tortured it into a sneer.

"I say you meant to drown me; and you sneer at me."

"We did not mean to drown you, sir," replied Tom Rush, respectfully.

"Yes, you did! And now you are laughing at your wicked deed," he replied, looking fiercely at me.

"I was laughing, Mr. Parasyte, to think that one whom we have just pulled out of the water should accuse us of attempting to drown him," I replied.

"That's what you meant to do; but you didn't dare to do it. You were afraid of the consequences."

"You are mistaken, sir; we had no such intentions," added Bob Hale, with due deference.

"Didn't you, or didn't Thornton, throw me over into the lake?" demanded he, as if surprised that we should attempt to deny the charge.

"No, sir; I did not," I answered.

"Didn't you turn your boat, and jerk the painter so as to throw me into the water?"

"I certainly changed the course of my boat, and that jerked the rope; but I did not intend to throw you into the water."

"Yes, you did! It is worse than folly for you to deny it!" replied he, angrily.

"If you had not been very careless, you could not have been thrown out!" I added.

"Don't tell me I was careless!"

"People acquainted with boats don't often stand up in them in such a sea as this, when they are towed."

"Let me hear no more of your impudence."

Discretion lay in silence, and we said no more. I ran the Splash up alongside the boat, from which Pearl and his companions had by this time dipped out all the water.

"Here is your boat, Mr. Parasyte," said Bob Hale. "Will you get into her, sir?"

"No, I will not," he replied.

"May I ask what you intend to do, sir?" I demanded, out of patience with him, in his unreasoning malice.

"You will take me to the shore."

"I will not," I replied, bluntly.

"You won't!"

"No, sir."

"We'll see," said he, rising to his feet.

"Better sit down, sir, or you will be overboard again," interposed Bob, as I drew the heavy tiller from its socket, intending to defend myself from assault.

The Splash lay with her sails shaking, and her position was a very uneasy one. Mr. Parasyte concluded to sit down, simply because he could not stand up, and I restored the tiller to the rudder.

"If you don't choose to get into that boat, Mr. Parasyte, I will land you at Cleaver Island," I added, as I filled away again, and headed the Splash towards the point indicated.

"Thornton, I want you to understand, that for all you have done you shall be brought to a strict account," said the principal, sternly, but vexed that he had failed to have his own way.

"I am ready to face the music, sir."

"No slang to me!"

"Will you land on Cleaver Island, or will you get into that boat?"

"I will get into the boat, but only - that I may the sooner bring you to justice," said he, desperately.

I came about again, and ran alongside of Pearl's boat. Mr. Parasyte, still dripping from his bath, embarked with his toadies.

"The end is not yet," said he, shaking his head, as the Splash filled away once more. "You will soon hear from me again."

We made no reply; and I was profoundly grateful that his life had been saved. My high hopes that what we had done for him might enable him to yield with better grace, and thus end the "breaking away," were dashed to the ground. With the wind on the beam, we ran by Cannondale, and stood down the lake near the shore, in search of the flat-boat, though it would be impossible for us to work her over to the island with the wind from the north-west.

"It is no use of talking any more," said Bob Hale, after a silence of several minutes. "I can never. go back to the Parkville Institute while Mr. Parasyte is the principal of it. He is too mean a man for me to sit under."

"My sentiments exactly," replied Tom Rush.

"I suppose I shall not go back, whoever is principal," I added.

"Why not?"

"I must take care of myself after this; and I can't afford to go to school."

"Perhaps your uncle will think better about it," suggested Tom.

"He may, but I don't believe he will."

"There's the flat-boat!" exclaimed one of our party forward.

"I see her; when the wind hauls round to the southward or eastward, we will come over, and work her back to the island," I replied. "She looks comfortable where she is, and we will return to our party."

In a short time the Splash reached the cove, where we found all our company assembled to learn the news, for they had observed our movements on the water. Vallington was much surprised when he learned that Mr. Parasyte was the person who had fallen overboard, and been rescued by the Splash. We told him what our persecutor intended to do with the steamer, and a council was immediately called to decide upon our proper course.

"What shall we do?" asked our general. "That's the question."

"I don't see that we can do anything," answered Bob Hale.

"Perhaps it will be best for us to keep still, and let things take their course," added Vallington.

"But Mr. Parasyte will carry off our tents and provisions," I interposed. "Can't we conceal our hams and other eatables."

"There comes the steamer!" shouted one of the boys.

"There isn't time now to do anything," continued

Vallington. "I will do the best I can for you, fellows."

Some proposed one thing, and some another; but it was plain that, in the multitude of advisers, nothing could be adopted which promised to help our prospects; and it was finally voted to leave the course of action entirely to our general, who had thus far proved himself worthy of confidence. He was to be guided entirely by circumstances; and he assured us he would be prompt to take advantage of any favorable event.

"Now, fellows, I want you all to keep together," said Vallington. "Don't one of you wander away from the rest. Leave all the talking to me — don't say a word to any one who comes in the steamer."

Our whole company promised to obey these instructions to the letter, and to be in readiness for any movement which might be ordered. The steamer ran up to the rude pier, and made fast her bow-line to a tree.

19*

222 BREAKING AWAY, OR

CHAPTER XX.

IN WHICH ERNEST TAKES THE WHEEL OF THE ADIENO.

WE watched with intense interest the proceedings of the men who came off in the steamer. After the exhibition of meanness on the part of Mr. Parasyte, it seemed that the rebellion was more serious than any of us had supposed. We made up our minds, with Bob Hale, that it would be impossible for us ever to be reconciled to him again. We felt as though the Rubicon had been passed, and what had commenced as a mere frolic was likely to end as a very grave affair. Though the boys talked solemnly at first about their rights, and had "struck" to vindicate a principle, they had no idea of the seriousness of their proceedings.

I shall not pretend to justify all that was done by our boys, or even to acknowledge that "breaking away," under any circumstances, is justifiable; but I do say, that such a man as the principal of the Parkville Liberal Institute was not a fit person to instruct and discipline young men. He was grossly unjust and partial; he was a tyrant at heart, though for policy's sake he veiled his purposes; he was low-minded and narrow in his views; and I am happy to say that he was not a fair specimen of the teachers of our land.

If the boys were wrong, he was so to a much greater degree, and his position and his influence made him responsible for the mischief he had driven the boys to perpetrate. It would have been better for them, as a body, to submit until redress could be obtained in a better way — as by the circular addressed to their parents, which was even then in the hands of the printer. I palliate, I do not justify, the conduct of the students.

Matters had begun to assume a graver aspect. Mr. Parasyte had come with a steamer, and with about a dozen men, as nearly as we could judge, to accomplish some purpose not yet apparent to us. We were curious to know whether we were to be driven like sheep on board of the Adieno, or whether our persecutor intended to resort to strategy. He had sent off his toadies to take our boats away; but he had started them while we were upon Cleaver Island, and before we had laid in our stock of provisions. This plan had failed. We were not long left in doubt.

Mr. Pararyte stepped on shore, followed by nine men, and then by the ten deserters from our camp. The men had sticks, bits of rope, and other articles in their hands. This looked like force, and we could not help glancing anxiously at Vallington, to ascertain, if we might, whether he intended to fight or to run away. We had no clubs or other weapons, but the pile of sticks which we had gathered for fuel was near. I saw the general glance at it; but I concluded that he did not intend to give battle, unless it was in self-defence.

As soon as the party under the lead of Mr. Parasyte had landed, the man who was left on board as boat-keeper hauled in the plank, by Mr. Parasyte's order, apparently to prevent the students from going on her deck. I could not but smile at this precaution, for the Adieno lay in such a position that the removal of the plank was no hinderance to agile boys like the students, and we could go on board when we chose.

Vallington stood on a stump near the path leading from the pier to the interior of the island, and his forces were gathered behind him, leaving the road open for the passage of the invaders.

Mr. Parasyte marched solemnly up the path, closely followed by the men and boys of his party. He looked uglier than I had ever seen him look before. By this time he must have been convinced that the Institute was ruined; that such a host of rebels could never be reduced to subjection; and he appeared to be acting out of the malice of his heart. But even then something was due to appearances, and he halted opposite the stump on which our general stood.

"Vallington!" said he, sharply and crustily.

"Sir."

"If you choose to go on board of that steamer, return to the Institute, and submit to the punishment you deserve, it is not too late for you to do so," continued Mr. Parasyte.

"Do you allude to me alone?"

"To all of you. I understand you to speak for the whole party."

"We shall be happy to do so," replied our general; and I am sure he spoke the sentiment of all the students.

"I am glad to see you are returning to reason," added the principal; but there was a look upon his face which showed how much pleasure he expected to derive from the proposed punishment.

"May I ask whether we are to be punished equally?" asked Vallington.

"You are to be punished in proportion to your offences — the ringleaders more, of course, than those who were simply led away by the influence of their leaders."

"And we are to be punished only for this breaking away?"

Mr. Parasyte bit his lips. It is possible he had a hope of restoring the Institute to its former condition.

"I don't understand you," said he.

"Is Thornton to be regarded as guilty only of breaking away, with the rest of us?"

"Thornton's affair is to be settled by itself," replied Mr. Parasyte.

"Then I have nothing more to say, sir," added Vallington, with becoming dignity.

I interposed, and begged him not to consider me, but to make terms if he could, and permit me to settle my own affair. Bob Hale and Tom Rush protested; but no protest was needed to keep Vallington true to his purpose.

"You reject my terms, Vallington," said Mr. Parasyte.

"I do, sir."

"I wish to do what I can to end this unhappy disturbance, and I am willing to say that the punishment shall be very mild — if you will return to your duty."

"You have treated one of our number with shameful injustice, Mr. Parasyte. We can prove, and have proved, that he was not guilty of the charge brought against him. If you will do him justice, and through him all the rest of us, we will submit to such punishment as you think proper for breaking away."

"Thornton!" exclaimed Mr. Parasyte, with a malignant sneer. "Do you expect me to receive the forced confession of Poodles and Pearl?"

"The confession was not forced, sir."

"Come here, Poodles," said the principal, sharply. Poodles stepped forward.

"Did you make this confession?" demanded Mr. Parasyte, sternly.

"I did — but I was afraid the fellows would kill me if I didn't do it," whined the toady.

"Do you hear that?"

"I hear it, and do not wonder at anything he says," replied Vallington.

Pearl told the same story; but our general protested that no compulsion had been used by the students; that two boys who were charged with deception were not to be believed in preference to eighty others. Vallington proposed that the case should be heard over again, and Poodles required to perform the examples. The principal was indignant, and refused all compromise.

"Thornton is not only guilty, but this very day he attempted to drown me in the lake," said he. "Do you think I can forgive him, without — "

"We don't ask you to forgive him, and he does not ask it. We only wish you to give him a fair trial."

"I will hear no more about it!" replied Mr. Parasyte, impatiently. "Will you return or not?"

"We will not."

"Very well. I wish every one here to understand that I have given you an opportunity to return to your duty. You will not, and the consequences be upon yourselves."

Mr. Parasyte walked up the path, followed by his party. As Pearl and Poodles passed us, a suggestion was made that we seize upon them, and punish them for the falsehoods they had uttered, and the meanness of which they had been guilty; but this proposition was promptly negatived by Vallington. We wondered what the invaders intended to do, and whether our general purposed to let them proceed without opposition. He stood calm and apparently unmoved on the stump, watching the enemy.

The principal halted his forces at the point where our provisions and cooking utensils were kept. Every eatable, and every utensil, even to the wooden

20

forks and spoons we had made, were seized and conveyed to the steamer. It was now clear that the
enemy did not mean to use force, unless we at-
tacked them. Mr. Parasyte intended to deprive us
of our food, and starve us into subjection. But he
was not satisfied yet; and when his party had deposited their burden on the deck of the steamer,
and the plank had again been hauled in, he marched
them by us once more.

"We shall soon see how long you will be willing to stay here," said our tyrant, as he walked
by the stump. "As Thornton said to the man in
charge of the boats at Cannondale, this morning,
I suppose I have a right to my own property,
wherever I find it."

"We paid for the provisions with our own money," replied Vallington.

Mr. Parasyte made no reply, but continued on
his way up the hill towards the tents. These also
he meant to take from us; and then, or in the
course of the day, he probably expected us to surrender, without conditions. The prospect did not
look pleasant, for we were to be without food or

shelter on the island. I was thinking how to save the Splash from capture, and I was about to suggest to Vallington that it would be better for me to put off in her, when our general spoke for himself.

The invaders were busily employed in striking the tents, and rolling up the canvas, about forty rods from where we stood. In a few moments they would be ready to put them on board of the steamer.

"Fellows," said Vallington, in a low and decided tone, "our time has come! We will take possession of that steamer. I have no idea of being starved into subjection. When I give the word, rush on board the best way you can."

"There's a man on her deck," said one of the boys; and we were all appalled at the boldness of the venture.

"Never mind him. Commodore Thornton, you will go to the wheel-house at once, and take the helm."

"Who will be engineer?" asked Tom Rush.

"I will be that myself. Bob Hale, you will run

the Splash out from the shore, and come on board when we are clear of the pier; take two good fellows with you. Are you all ready?"

"All ready!" replied the boys; and the voices of some trembled.

"Forward then!" shouted Vallington; and he leaped from the stump, and ran down to the wharf, followed by the whole company.

Bob Hale got into the Splash with two boys, and pushed her off. The rest of us leaped over the bulwarks, scrambled up to the hurricane deck, or rushed in at the gangway. Vallington cast off the bowline himself, just as I reached the wheel-house.

"Back her!" I shouted; and the word was passed through the boys to Vallington, who had now gone to the engine-room.

We were not a moment too quick, for just as the steamer began to back from the pier, the invaders, laden with canvas and poles, appeared on the wharf.

CHAPTER XXI.

IN WHICH ERNEST CONTINUES TO ACT AS PILOT OF THE STEAMER.

WHEN I reached the deck of the Adieno I met the person who was in charge of the steamer. It was the lame man who had disputed my right to the Splash in the morning, and to whom we had given two dollars. He looked astonished at the sudden movement of the students, but he offered no resistance; and, without waiting to hear what he had to say, I ran up the ladder to the wheel-house, leaving Tom Rush to settle all questions in dispute with him.

My heart bounded with excitement as we carried out our desperate enterprise, and I gave Henry Vallington credit for more daring and courage than I had ever supposed him to possess. He seemed to me just then to be a general indeed, and to be bet-

20 *

ter fitted to fight his way through an enemy's country than to become a parson.

"Back her!" I shouted, almost beside myself with excitement, as I saw Mr. Parasyte and his heavily-laden followers rushing down to the pier.

My words were repeated by the boys on the forward deck, and Vallington hastened to the engine-room. I heard the hissing steam as it rushed through the cylinders, and without knowing what was going to happen next, — whether or not the boiler would explode, and the deck be torn up beneath me, — I waited in feverish anxiety for the result. Then I heard the splash of the wheels; the crank turned, rumbled, and jarred on its centre, but went over, and continued to turn. The Adieno moved, and the motion sent a thrill through my whole being. It was fortunate for us that she lay at the pier in such a position as to require no special skill in handling her. The open lake was astern of her, with clear sailing for two miles.

I was not a steamboat man; I had never even steered any craft with a wheel, and I did not feel at all at home. But I had often been up and down

the lake in this very steamer, and being of an inquiring mind, I had carefully watched the steers-
man. It had always looked easy enough to me,
and I always believed I could do it as well as
anybody else. I tried to keep cool, and I think
I looked cool to others; but I was extremely nervous. I did not exactly know which way to turn
the wheel.

When I found there were no obstructions astern
of the steamer, I brought the flagstaff on the bow
into range with the end of the pier, — or rather I
found them in range, — and with these to guide me,
I soon learned by experience which way to turn the
wheel; and the moment I got the hang of the thing,
I had confidence enough to offer my services to pilot
any steamer all over the lake. The paddles kept
slapping the water, and the boat continued to back
until she was a quarter of a mile from the land, when
I thought it was time to come about, and go forward instead of backward. There were two bell-pulls
on the wheel-frame, and at a venture I pulled
one of them. I did not know whether Vallington
understood the bells or not; but there was only one

thing to be done in this instance, and he did it —
he stopped the machinery.

After pausing a moment for the steamer to lose
her sternway, I rang the other bell, intending to have
her go ahead; but the engineer did not heed my
summons. A moment afterwards Vallington appeared
on the forward deck, wiping from his brow the perspiration, which indicated that the engine-room was
a hot place, or that his mental struggles were very
severe.

" What was that last bell for ? " he asked, hailing
me in the wheel-house.

" To go ahead," I replied.

" You haven't got the hang of the bells, commodore," said he, with a smile; " but come down, and
we will talk the matter over, and find out what we
are going to do."

I went down to the forward deck, quite as anxious as any one else to know what was to be done,
for it seemed to me that we had " drawn an ele-
phant " as a prize. When I reached the deck, Vallington was writing with his pencil, and handed me
the paper as I joined him.

" Here are your directions, Mr. Pilot," said he.

" I know the lake, but I never had any experience in a steamer," I replied, in self-defence, as I read the paper, on which was written : —

" *One bell — ahead, slowly.*

Two bells — stop.

Three bells — back.

Four bells — ahead, full speed."

"There are two bell-pulls in the wheel-house," I added.

" You pulled the right one the first time; the other is for the men to shift the chain-box," he replied. " Now, fellows, what shall we do? is the next question."

Nobody seemed to know what we were to do; and all were quite willing to leave the question with our bold general.

" Where is the lame man who had charge of the steamer ?" he asked.

" I have fixed him," answered Tom Rush, with a significant smile.

" How have you fixed him ?"

" I told him we should throw him overboard if

he didn't keep quiet, and gave him three dollars I picked up among the fellows."

Tom was fit to be a member of the diplomatic corps — bully and bribe in the same breath! Probably the lame man, who was only a deck hand, employed but for that day, was not disposed to make any very active opposition to our plans. At any rate, he sat on the chain-box as contented as though everything was going on regularly on board of the boat. Mr. Parasyte had pressed all hands into his service, even to the captain and engineer, in bringing off the provisions and tents. I suppose that it never occurred to the principal, or to the officers of the boat, that a crowd of boys would attempt such a desperate enterprise as the capture of the Adieno, or they would have taken some precautions to avoid such an event. It is not strange that they did not think of such a thing, for if it had been proposed to me beforehand, I should as soon have thought of carrying off the island as the steamer.

Mr. Parasyte, the captain, and engineer stood on the edge of the pier. The principal looked astonished and overwhelmed; the captain was gesticulating violently to us; and the rest of the party looked like so many statues. There was no remedy for their misfortune; they had no boat, and could do nothing. Mr. Parasyte now had the same pleasant prospect which he had spread out before us — that of staying on Pine Island without food till some one came to his assistance. We hoped he enjoyed it; and in the mean time we turned our attention to our own immediate future.

"Fellows, I am afraid we have got into a bad scrape," said Vallington, again wiping his heated brow; and we could not help seeing that he did not feel just right in view of what he had done.

"All right; we will take our chances," replied one of the students; and this was the prevailing sentiment.

"Although I think we were right in the beginning, I am afraid we are overdoing the matter. But what could we do?" continued our general, with energy. "We couldn't stay on that island and be starved out. We paid for the provisions with our own money, and they had no right to take them from us."

"No!" shouted the boys, indignantly.

"Now we have the steamer; what shall we do with her?"

"Let us go on a cruise," suggested Fred Mason.

"I did not take possession of the boat with the intention of making any use of her only to get away from the island while it was possible to do so," replied Vallington.

"O, let's have some fun in her, now we have got her," added Mason.

"We are drifting over to Cannondale pretty rapidly, general," I interposed. "We must go ahead, or we shall run ashore."

"I don't exactly know what to do, or where to go," continued our perplexed leader.

"We must go ahead now, and settle that question by and by," I added.

"Can you steer her, commodore?" he asked.

"Certainly I can. I understand the wheel now, and I know all about the lake. If you can manage the engine, I can take care of the steering."

"My brother is an engineer on a Hudson River boat, and I have spent many a day with him in the engine-room. I think I understand the engine pretty well," he replied.

"Let us go ahead then," said one of the impatient fellows.

"We will start her again, commodore; and I wish you would take her to some place where we can lie to, and decide upon our future course."

"I will do so, general; but I don't think it will hurt those on the island to wait a while," I answered.

"Very well; we will go where you pilot us, commodore," added Vallington, as he returned to the engine-room.

Three of the students were sent down into the fire-room, after being instructed in their duty by the general, who was careful to tell them not to put too much wood in the furnaces. By this time the Splash had come alongside, and was made fast to the stern. I invited Bob Hale and Tom Rush to occupy the wheel-house with me, and I took my place at the spokes.

"What are we going to do?" asked Bob, who had not been present at the conference on the forward deck.

"That is not decided," replied Tom. "We are

21

going to lie to somewhere, and talk the matter over."

"I don't know about this steaming it on the lake," added Bob, shaking his head. "Suppose the boat should burst her boiler — where should we be?"

"No danger of that; Vallington knows all about engines, and the commodore knows how to steer," said Tom, lightly.

I struck one bell, after looking at the paper which Vallington had given me, to make sure that I was right. In response to my signal, the wheels began to turn, and the Adieno went "ahead slowly." I soon brought her to bear on the helm, and finding I had the boat under perfect control, I ventured to strike the four bells, which indicated that she was to "go ahead, full speed."

The steam was rather low in the boilers, and "full speed" I found was not very rapid. The boat steered easily, and minded her helm so promptly, that I soon became quite fascinated with my occupation. There was something very exhilarating in the fact that I was directing the course of what to me was an immense craft; and every time I moved the wheel, and

saw the bow veer in obedience to her helm, it afforded me a thrill of delight, and I wholly forgot
the enormity of the enterprise in which our party
were engaged. I was so pleased with my employ-
ment that I came very near devoting my life to the
business of piloting a steamboat.

I steered the Adieno to the northward, until she
had passed clear of Pine Island, when I put her
head to the west, intending to run for a couple
of islands six miles down the lake, called "The
Sisters."

CHAPTER XXII.

IN WHICH ERNEST PILOTS THE ADIENO TO "THE SISTERS."

THERE comes the Champion!" exclaimed Bob Hale, pointing to the steamer that regularly made her trip round the lake every day, as she came out from behind a point of land on the north shore, beyond which she made a landing.

"We must give her a wide berth," I replied.

"Why so? Her people will not know that it isn't all right with the Adieno."

"We are in no immediate danger; but suppose the captain of this boat should find means to get to Cannondale before the Champion does, he might engage her to go in pursuit of us."

"That would be jolly!" said Tom Rush. "We should have a glorious race!"

"But the chances are against us in a race," I

replied, confounded by the temerity of Tom in thinking of such a thing as contending with the steamboat men on their own ground.

"Not a bit of it, Ernest. The Adieno is the faster boat of the two — that has been tried a dozen times," added Tom, as much excited as though the race had actually commenced.

"We must not attempt to beard the lion in his den."

"Why not? We might as well be hung for an old sheep as a lamb. We are in a scrape, and even Vallington thinks it is a bad one by this time. The more advantage we gain, the better terms we can make."

"I don't know about it, Tom. I feel as though we had carried this thing about far enough, and the sooner we get out of the scrape, the better it will be for us."

"Those are my sentiments. My father is part owner in this boat, and I think he will not enjoy the idea of our going off on a cruise in her," added Bob Hale.

"Pooh! we won't hurt her," replied Tom.

21 *

"We don't intend to hurt her; but we are following a business just now that we don't know much about."

"Don't you know the lake, and don't Vallington know all about the engine?"

"Neither of us has had any experience."

"That's so," added Bob. "In my opinion breaking away is about played out. We have made up our minds that we can't have anything more to do with Mr. Parasyte, and we may as well return to Parkville, and go to work in a more reasonable way. We can send the circulars to our parents, and dig out of the difficulty the best way we can."

"I agree to that," I answered. Not that I cared for myself, for my "breaking away" was a much more serious matter than that of my fellow-students; but I thought it better for them to get out of the mud before they sank any deeper into the mire.

"I am willing to do as the rest of the fellows do; but I don't want to be whipped round a stump when there is no need of it," continued

Tom. "If the Champion chases us, I go for keeping out of the way till we can retire from the field without any broken heads."

"So far I shall agree with you, Tom," I replied. "I am not in favor of surrendering, to be kicked and cuffed by these steamboat men, who are not exactly lambs in their dispositions."

"What's the use of talking?" interposed Bob Hale. "The Champion is not after us, and it does not appear that she will be."

"It appears so to me," I answered. "I have no idea that the captain of the Adieno will stay on Pine Island all day. I found a way to get ashore this morning, and I think he will be able to do so."

"Perhaps he will."

"I am perfectly satisfied that he will reach the shore by one o'clock, if he has not already done so. No doubt he thinks his boat will be smashed to pieces, or blown up, if he does not recover her soon. He isn't going to sit down and bite his finger nails."

"He may not be able to get the Champion," replied Bob Hale, who evidently did not wish to believe that there would be a contest for superiority between the two steamers.

"I don't profess to be a prophet, Bob, but I can see through a millstone when the hole is big enough. I will tell you just how I *think* it will be. The captain of the Adieno will make a raft, and get to Cannondale. Then he will take the Champion for Parkville, arriving about half past one. The boat does not start on her trip down the lake till five o'clock, and that will give her three hours and a half to spare. You may take my word for it, that time will be used in chasing us."

"Very likely you are right, Ernest; we shall see. It is twelve o'clock now, and we haven't much time to consider what we shall do," said Bob Hale, looking very serious; and it was evident now, if it had not been before, that he had strong objections to any steamboat enterprises.

"It's nearly dinner time," added Tom; "and I must go and see about the provender."

Bob Hale went below to have a talk with Vallington, and the commissary left for the kitchen, to provide our noon rations. I was left alone in the wheel-house. I enjoyed my occupation very much; but the talk of my friends had filled me with doubts and fears, so that my situation was not so delightful as before. I could not help asking myself what was to come out of this scrape, and it seemed to me that it could result in nothing but defeat and disaster.

The Adieno was approaching The Sisters, at one of which there was a pier, like that at Pine Island, which had been erected for the use of the scows employed in the transportation of the wood cut on the island. I knew that the water around it was deep enough for the steamer, for I had seen her land there. Between the two islands there was a channel not more than twenty rods wide, by which alone the wood pier could be reached.

The channel had barely depth enough in the middle to permit the passage of the Adieno; but as it was perfectly straight, and the water high in the lake, I considered myself competent to take her through. The boat minded her helm very prettily, and there was no current in the channel to interfere with my calculations, so that I did not regard the place as very difficult navigation. I had been through the channel twenty times in the Splash. The pier ran out from the island to the deep water, so that I had only to run the bow up to it, and make fast to the ring. The steamer would be safe here, and, being concealed between the islands, could only be seen from one point above and one below; and here we could have our dinner, and hold our important consultation without the danger of interruption.

I had another and stronger motive for entering this channel, and without which, perhaps, I might not have had the confidence to run even the slight risk which the navigation of the passage involved. It was so fully ground into my bones that the Champion would be after us about three o'clock, or as soon as she had landed her passengers at Parkville, that I wished to be fully prepared for any emergency. To the north of the "North Sister," and to the south of the "South Sister," the water was shoal for a mile in each direction, while the channel between the islands seemed to have been kept open by the strong south-west and north-east winds, as they forced the waters through. At any rate, there was a channel with five feet of water in it, though I was not entirely certain in regard to the explanation of the fact.

The Champion was a larger boat, drawing one foot more water aft than the Adieno, and therefore could not pass through the channel, or come within half a mile of the wood pier. My idea was, that in this position we could not be approached by our anticipated pursuer, as we lay moored at the wharf. If chased, I might be able to gain on the Champion by running through The Sisters Channel, which would enable me to come out two or three miles ahead of her on the opposite side, as she would be obliged to go a mile, north or south, to get round the shoal water.

I was so pleased with the calculation I had made, that I could not help wishing I was employed in a better cause than in fighting the battle of a parcel of runaway students, — it would have been so exciting to play the game of strategy in real earnest, and in a good cause. I plumed myself just then on being a great navigator, and a shrewd calculator, and I wished to test my plans. It so happened, however, that they were tested, as the sequel will show.

The Adieno approached the narrow channel, which was just as clearly defined in my mind as though the bottom of the lake had been laid bare to me; for I had always been obliged to keep in the deep water even when I went through in the Splash. As the wind, though not so strong as it had been in the morning, still came fresh from the north-west, I hugged the weather side of the channel, and, with the boat at full speed, went on my course. I was just on the point of ringing one bell to slow down, when the steamer's wheels suddenly stopped.

"What are you about, Thornton?" shouted Vallington, rushing out of the engine-room to the forward deck, both excited and angry.

"I'm all right!" I replied, provoked at his singular conduct in stopping the boat at such a critical point.

"Where are you going? Do you want to run us all ashore?"

"*I* don't, but I think *you* do. Go ahead, or we

shall be aground in a moment," I added, as the Adieno was losing her headway, and we were not yet sheltered by the North Sister from the force of the wind.

"I'm not going any farther into this hole," replied he, sternly. "I think you are crazy, Thornton, to take the boat into such a place."

"I know what I am about," I answered, rather sharply; "and if you will take care of the engine, I will look out for the helm."

"You'll smash the boat all to pieces—going into a little, narrow, dirty channel at full speed."

"I know the channel as well as I know my own name. If you will go ahead, we shall be all right!" I shouted.

"I won't go ahead any farther into this hole," said he, decidedly.

"O, yes, go ahead," interposed Bob Hale. "Ernest knows what he is about."

"Perhaps he does; but I want to know what he is about too. I don't want the steamer smashed or injured."

It was of no use for me to say anything more,

22

and I held my tongue.   The Adieno had now entirely lost her headway, and as the strong wind began to act on her top works, she drifted over to the
lee side of the channel.   She grated a moment on
the bottom, and then stuck fast, hard aground, so far
as I could judge.

"There! now do you see what you have done?"
shouted Vallington, stamping his foot angrily upon
the deck.

"I see what *you* have done," I replied, as calmly
as I could; and that was not saying much, for I was
very indignant at being charged with what was
plainly his doing.

And there we were, hard and fast aground, with
a tempest brewing between the general and the commodore.

CHAPTER XXIII.

IN WHICH ERNEST TAKES COMMAND OF THE EXPEDITION.

IT was useless for me to remain any longer in the wheel-house, and I descended by the forward ladder to the deck. I was indignant, but I was determined to "face the music." The best of friends are liable to "fall out" at times, and no better than Vallington and myself had ever existed. He was burdened by the responsibility of the position he had assumed, and perhaps did not feel just right about the course he had taken. These things may have made him irritable. Though I had never before known him to be unkind or uncourteous, he had certainly "pitched into me," on the present occasion, in a manner which my self-respect would not permit me to endure.

I had been acting, in charge of the wheel, to the

best of my ability; and I was perfectly confident
that nothing would have gone wrong with the steamer
if the engineer had not stopped the wheels.   However I felt on the general question of duty, I was
quite satisfied that I had been faithful to the interests of the expedition upon which we had embarked;
and I could not bear to be "snapped up," and treated
like an inferior in knowledge and skill, even by my
chosen leader.   I was "chief of navigation," at least;
and I felt that the general had interfered with my
part of the work.   He accused me of causing the
mischief, when he had been the author of it himself; and this was so plain to me that I could
not help resenting it.

Very likely my face was flushed with anger and
excitement when I confronted Vallington on the forward deck.   If it was, his was not less so, and there
was a lively prospect of a "family quarrel."   With
my strong consciousness that I had done right, or,
at least, intended to do right, so far as our expedition was concerned, I could have afforded to refrain
from heated expressions; and it would have been
better if I had done so.   It is no reason, because

one person gets mad, that another should. It is more dignified, manly, and Christian for one always to control his temper. Let the truth be spoken forcibly, if need be, but kindly.

"We are in for a pretty scrape now," said Vallington, sternly and angrily, as I walked up to him.

"It isn't my fault if we are," I answered, sharply.

"Why do you say it isn't your fault, Thornton? Didn't you pilot the steamer into this hole?"

"I didn't pilot her aground. When you stopped her there were two or three feet of water under her keel."

"What did you bring her in here for? If I hadn't stopped her when I did, you would have smashed her up."

"Perhaps I should," I answered with a sneer, when I found it was impossible to make any headway against the general's unreasonable speech.

"You were going at full speed; and it is lucky I happened to see the shore and stop her when I did."

"I have nothing more to say," I replied, seating myself on the rail of the steamer.

22 *

"I don't think there is much more to be said. Here we are, hard aground; and anybody that has a mind to come after us can take us."

I made no reply. Vallington went to the gangway and looked over into the shallow water. Then he walked over to the other side, and I had no doubt our situation looked hopeless to him. After he had walked about a while, his anger abated; and perhaps he was conscious that he had been too fast in expressing himself.

"What's to be done? That's the next question," said he.

"I suppose nothing can be done," replied Tom Rush, who was more disappointed than any other fellow on board. "They say the Champion will be down after us this afternoon. Perhaps she will drag us off, and then our tyrants will treat us as they think proper."

"You needn't disturb yourselves about the Champion," I interposed. "She can't come within half a mile of us at least."

"Is that so?"

"That is so."

"It doesn't make much difference whether she can or not. We must stay here till some one helps us out of the scrape," added Vallington. "It was stupid to come in here."

"I don't think so," said Bob Hale, decidedly. "Here we are aground, anyhow."

"Harry," continued Bob, gently and kindly, "I think Ernest was right in what he said. If you hadn't stopped the engine, we should have gone through well enough."

Vallington bit his lips, and he and Bob walked aft together. They were absent a few moments; and when he returned, the general's face wore a different expression.

"Thornton, I acknowledge that I was wrong," said he, extending his hand to me.

The boys standing around us immediately began to clap their hands in token of their satisfaction. In matters of navigation they were more willing to believe in me than in Vallington; and probably most of them were satisfied that I had been in the right.

"Don't say another word," I replied, jumping down from my seat, and grasping his offered hand.

"You will excuse my hasty language," he continued.

"Certainly; and I ask the same favor of you," I replied.

"I irritated you, commodore, by my unreasonable words, and I am willing to bear all the blame."

"You don't deserve it all."

If Vallington had been less noble and manly, we might have had a bad quarrel; as it was, our differences were promptly healed.

"Now, what's to be done, commodore?" the general proceeded. "I have got you into the scrape; but I hope you will be able to get out of it."

"I think I shall," I replied, confidently.

"They say we are to be chased by the Champion this afternoon; but just now we don't seem to be in condition to be chased even by a scow."

"We are not very hard aground; we only drifted on the shoal bottom; and if I mistake not, we can work her off. So far as the Champion is concerned, I am satisfied she will be after us as soon as she has landed her passengers at Parkville; but that will not be for a couple of hours yet."

" Then you really expect her."

" I certainly do ; and when we float again, I don't care how soon she comes. I came into this place, which you call a hole, general, simply to get ready for the Champion ; for she draws too much water to pass through this channel."

" Well, that's a double proof that I have wronged you, and I am all the more sorry for my unkindness."

" Don't mention that again, Vallington," I replied, touched by his magnanimity.

" Fellows," said Vallington, turning to the boys, " I resign my commission as general-in-chief of this expedition."

" No, no!" shouted the students.

" We are on the water now, and it is more proper that the commodore should have the entire command. When we are on shore again, I will resume my office. I will obey all the commodore's orders now, and the rest of you will do the same."

I protested, but the general insisted. We finally agreed to the proposition, and for the time I became the commander of the expedition. Our first business was to float the steamer. Vallington went back to the engine-room, and I resumed my place at the wheel. I rang to back her, and the paddles slapped the water furiously for a time, but without producing any effect. The steamer had taken the ground harder than I supposed. She had run her bow upon the gradual slope of the bottom till the wheels were powerless to move her.

The boys looked at one another in blank dismay, and seemed to feel just as though the enemy were to "bag" them, as a sportsman does the game he has brought down. I did not despair yet. From the wheel-house I had surveyed the surroundings, and a plan had occurred to me by which I hoped to work the Adieno out of her uncomfortable position.

"No go," said Vallington, as we met together on the main deck.

"Not yet; but we won't give it up. The bow had dug into the bottom more than I supposed. We must carry a line ashore, and make fast to one of those trees; then I think we can pull her off."

Bob Hale, with two others, was sent ashore on the North Sister in the Splash, carrying the end of a long rope. When he had secured it to a large tree on the shore, I took the other end, the line passing through a round hawse-hole forward, and conveyed it aft to the shaft. After winding it four or five times round the shaft, I told the boys to haul it taut; and about twenty of them laid hold of the rope to "take in the slack," if we were fortunate enough to obtain any.

"Bully for you," said Vallington, as he comprehended my arrangement.

"If the rope don't break, something will come," I replied.

I had been obliged to join several ropes, in order to form one long enough; but having carefully avoided "granny knots," I hoped it would hold. The bearing of the line was at the hawse-hole, near the bow of the boat; and as the power was applied to the rope by turning the wheel and shaft, the tendency was to haul the forward end of the boat off the ground into the deeper water.

"All ready now, Vallington," I continued, when the preparations were completed. "Back her slowly."

He started the engine, as I directed.

"Haul taut on that rope!" I shouted to the boys at the line.

The wheels turned, and the shaft revolved. The rope groaned and strained.

"Stop her!" I added to the engineer, afraid to risk the strain. "Run aft the chain-box."

My orders were obeyed; and as the boat floated at her stern, the weight of the chain-box was sensibly felt.

"Back her slowly again," I continued.

Again the rope groaned and strained as though too much was expected of it.

"She starts!" cried the boys forward. "She is coming off!"

I heard the keel scraping upon the bottom; and as the rope wound up, the Adieno slid off into the deep water.

"Hurrah!" shouted the boys.

"Let go the rope!" I called to the boys aft. "Stop her, Vallington."

I hastened up to the wheel-house, the better to work her. I found she lay in good position to go ahead, and I shouted to Bob Hale to cast off the rope from the tree, directing the boys on the forward deck to haul it on board. I rang one bell, and the boat moved ahead slowly towards the wood pier. The boys cheered lustily, and were overjoyed at our good fortune in getting out of the scrape. In a few moments I ran the bow of the steamer up to the pier, and she was made fast to the ring.

"Now we are all hunky-dory," said Tom Rush, who was rather given to "expressions," and who was over-joyed to find there was still a chance for an excitement.

"Not quite," I added.

"What's the matter now?"

"We want some dinner."

"You shall have it in half an hour."

And while Tom was superintending the cooking, Vallington, Bob Hale, and myself had a consultation in the wheel-house.

23

CHAPTER XXIV.

IN WHICH ERNEST ENGAGES IN AN EXCITING STEAM-BOAT RACE.

IF you ask for my opinion," said Bob Hale, "I say we had better return to Parkville at once, and not wait to be driven back."

"It is easy enough for you to say that," replied Tom Rush, who had joined us. "You live there, and all you have to do is to go home; but what are the fellows who reside a hundred miles from there to do?"

"They will not be any worse off there than they will be here. The question is only between going back and being driven back," added Bob.

"I suppose that we are to acknowledge that breaking away has been a failure," said Vallington.

"Not at all; I, for one, won't have any more to do with Mr. Parasyte," answered Bob. "What do you say, Ernest?"

"I probably shall not go back to the Institute, whatever happens," I replied. "My breaking away is not from school only, but from all the home I ever knew. I have been thrown out upon the world, to take care of myself."

For a moment my friends seemed to forget that we were in council to determine what should be done for the rebels in their sympathy for me; but I assured them I was not at all concerned about myself, and felt abundantly able to make my way without any help.

"But what an old humbug your uncle is!" said Tom.

"He is a strange man. He seemed to have turned me out because I displeased him in resisting Mr. Parasyte's injustice. He is afraid my conduct will lessen the value of his mortgage on the Parkville Liberal Institute."

"I think Mr. Parasyte's conduct has lessened it," said Vallington. "But all this is neither here nor there. What shall we do with this steamer?"

"Take her back to Parkville, and leave her there," answered Bob.

" What are the fellows to do?" asked Tom.

"Let them go back to the Institute, and lie back till something happens."

"I don't believe anything will happen this year," laughed Tom, who was always light-hearted in any emergency.

" Now, I think something will happen within a few days. I know that certain persons in Parkville, who have long been dissatisfied with Mr. Parasyte, intended to have a change months ago; and if I mistake not, this affair of ours will bring matters to a head," said Bob.

" What can they do? Mr. Parasyte is as obstinate as a mule, and owns the Institute himself," added Vallington.

"Not quite; my uncle will own the most of it if his note isn't paid," I interposed.

"I am not at liberty to tell even what I know, which is not much; but I believe something will turn up which will put things right at the Institute. All we have to do is to go back to Parkville and make our peace with the steamboat folks the best way we can," continued Bob.

We all agreed that the steamboat enterprise was
a bad affair for us; but we were just as unanimous
in the opinion that we could not have done otherwise than take her as we did. It was mean of her
captain to lend himself and his boat to such a man
as Mr. Parasyte. We could not stay on Pine Island
without food and without shelter. But we hoped
to return the Adieno uninjured, and, through the
powerful influence of Bob Hale's father, who was the
wealthiest man in the county, to escape without any
serious consequences. It was decided, therefore, to
return to Parkville just as soon as we had eaten our
dinner.

Tom Rush's cooks were either very dilatory, or
they had not got the hang of the steamer's kitchen,
for we had to wait an hour for the meal. We
dined in the cabin, where we found everything we
needed to set the table; and in spite of the desperate condition of our affairs, we enjoyed ourselves
very much. Some one ventured to inquire if we
could not charter the Adieno for a week, and finish
our breaking away in her, it would be so pleasant
to live on board, and cruise up and down the beau-

23 *

tiful lake. But it was satisfactorily shown that our finances, however they might be improved by letters from home, would not warrant such a piece of extravagance.

This was the last day of the breaking away, at least on the lake and in camp, and we were disposed to make the most of it. As soon as it was announced that we were to return to Parkville, though some of the students murmured, and wished to make a trip down the lake before we went back, the plan was accepted, and the boys were disposed to improve the remainder of the cruise. They persisted in enjoying it; and before the boat left the wood pier, they were skylarking and training as though the future would require no account to be rendered of their past conduct.

Vallington went to the engine-room, and directed the boys below to start up the fires. With Bob Hale I went to the wheel-house; while Tom Rush, as he had been directed by our chief, had all the dishes washed, and everything put in order in the cabin and kitchen, for we wished to leave the boat in as good condition in every respect as we found her.

"Cast off the fasts!" I called to the boys on the forward deck, when Vallington informed me that he had steam enough.

"All clear!" replied those who were doing duty as deck hands.

I rang to back her; and when the bow of the Adieno was clear of the wharf, I started her forward slowly; and keeping her in the middle of the channel, she passed in safety out into the broad lake.

"We are too late; we ought to have gone before," said Bob, impatiently. "There comes the Champion. I was certain she would be after us — as certain as you were. What shall we do?"

I headed the Adieno down the lake when I saw the Champion — that is, away from Parkville.

"We must take our chances; we can't do anything else," I replied to Bob, as I threw the wheel over.

"But you are not headed for Parkville."

"Not yet; for I don't mean to be captured."

"How can you help it?"

"Perhaps I can't help it; but I can try."

I notified Vallington through the speaking-tube that the Champion was in sight, and headed towards us.

"We mustn't let her overtake us, if we can help it. I will put on the steam," he replied.

"All right; I can keep out of her way," I answered.

"Why not surrender?" said Bob, who stood at my side watching the Champion.

"Surrender!" I exclaimed.

"Why not? What harm will it do?"

"I have no idea of throwing myself into the hands of those steamboat men. Don't you see the Champion is full of men?"

"Do you suppose they would harm us?"

"I do. No doubt Mr. Parasyte is on board, and he will give them liberty to maul us as much as they please."

"Perhaps you are right; I didn't think of Mr. Parasyte's being with them."

"Of course he is; and I think we can make better terms by fighting it out. For my own part, I would run the steamer ashore and take to the woods, rather than give myself up to Mr. Parasyte and such a gang as he has now."

Bob did not fully agree with me, though he thought

we had better get back to Parkville, if we could. This was not an easy matter, for the Champion lay between us and our destination, and could cut us off if we attempted to pass her. She could run up alongside of the Adieno, if we attempted to dodge her, and throw her men on our decks.

The Sisters lay near the middle of the lake, and the Champion must go to the north or to the south of them. I made a blunder; I ought to have waited at the end of the channel until our pursuer had reached his most southern or most northern point in coming round the shoal, and then gone off in the opposite direction; but even then he might have put about, and headed us off. It was hard to decide what to do, and I continued to go to the westward until the Champion, which had chosen the southern passage, was due south of The Sisters, when I stood away to the northward.

But the pursuer "had me;" and finding it was useless to attempt to get by her, I headed the boat down the lake again. The Champion then crowded on all steam and chased us. This was exactly what I wished her to do, and I led her five miles down the lake.

"I don't know about it, Ernest," said Bob, shaking his head. "I think she will catch us. This boat is the fastest, but we don't understand her well enough to make her do her best."

"I am afraid of that; but don't talk to me, if you please, now," I replied.

I led the Champion to the northward of an island at this point; and here her captain made a blunder, which restored to me the advantage I had lost before. When the Champion was well by the island, I turned the Adieno to the southward, and went round the island, which prevented our pursuer from cutting us off, and saving any of the distance, as he might have done, in the open lake.

"There, Bob, I have done it now, and I am satisfied," I said. "She can't cut us off, and it will be a square race up the lake."

"The Champion is gaining on us every moment," replied Bob.

The other steamer was certainly overhauling us. The superior skill of the men in charge of her gave them the advantage. I told Vallington of the fact, and soon the roaring of the furnaces and the creak-

CHAMPION.

ing of the boat assured me he was in earnest. But in spite of his renewed exertions, the Champion was gaining a little, and I was sure that she would overtake us long before we could reach Parkville. I headed her for The Sisters, therefore, determined to put in force the plan I had devised before dinner. I ran directly for the channel, and the Champion followed.

The pursuer was almost upon us when we came within a quarter of a mile of the end of the channel. Both boats were shaking and trembling under the high pressure of steam, and every fellow on board the Adieno was in a fever of excitement.

" Crowd her, Vallington ! " I shouted through the tube.

" The Champion's bow is within ten feet of us ! " exclaimed Bob.

" Stop her, you villains ! " cried the captain of the boat from the bow of the Champion.

" Give it to her, Vallington ! In two minutes more we are safe ! " I yelled through the tube.

" She is almost upon us ! " said Bob, tremulously.

At that moment we heard the engine bell of the

Champion ring, as the Adieno approached the narrow channel. Her wheels stopped, and she began to back vigorously.

"Give them three cheers!" I called to the students, as the pursuer backed out; and they were given with a will.

CHAPTER XXV.

IN WHICH ERNEST PILOTS THE ADIENO TO PARKVILLE.

THE Champion could not pass through the narrow and shoal channel between The Sisters, and my calculation had been correct. I was so elated at the victory that I could not refrain from calling for the cheers, though it was bad policy for us to crow over such rivals. A moment before, the nerves of all on board of the Adieno had been strained to their utmost tension by the exciting peril of the moment. The bow of our pursuer had actually lapped over the stern of our steamer, and we expected the captain of the Adieno, who stood on the rail, holding on to an awning stanchion, would leap on board of us, after he had bawled himself hoarse in ordering us to stop.

The pilot of the Champion was evidently the coolest man in the steamer, and he had run her to the

24

very mouth of The Sisters Channel; but he knew that she could not go through, and at the last practicable instant, he had "stopped" and "backed," leaving the victory with us. It was a tremendous relief when the pressure was removed from our overstrained nerves; and never were cheers given more enthusiastically, even madly, than those which saluted the people of the Champion at the dawn of our triumph.

The Adieno had entered the narrow channel, and I doubt not her appalled captain on the deck of the other boat expected to see her "take the ground" and be smashed to pieces. The moment I saw the pursuer was backing out, I rang to stop her, and then to go ahead slowly; for I had no more idea of smashing her than I had of smashing my own head.

"Silence, now!" I shouted to the boys on deck, who were still yelling to the utmost capacity of their lungs; for I was afraid the noise might drown the sound of the bell in the engine-room, in case I had occasion to ring it.

The students hushed up instantly. They had

climbed upon the rails, and secured other positions where they could obtain a view of our discomfited pursuer; and a more excited and delighted set of fellows never gathered on the deck of a steamer.

"Have your eye on the Champion, Bob, and tell me what she does," said I to my companion in the wheel-house; for I needed both of my own eyes to keep the Adieno in the channel, where a slight mistake on my part would have ruined all my plans, and perhaps the steamer in which we sailed.

"I will," replied he.

"What is she doing?"

"Nothing."

"Don't she move?"

"No — she hasn't started yet. They probably expect us to go ashore before we get through the channel."

"Well, the longer she waits there, the better for us, for she can't come through," I added.

The Adieno passed safely through the channel, and came out into the broad lake beyond The Sisters. I rang to go ahead at full speed again, for we had now a clear run to Parkville before us.

"The Champion has started her wheels again, Ernest," said Bob Hale, as I rang the bell; "she is backing out of the inlet into the open lake."

"All right — let her back. We have a good three miles the start of her, and she can't catch us before we get to Parkville," I replied.

I informed Vallington through the speaking tube in regard to the situation, with which he was entirely satisfied. I asked him to keep the boat moving at her best pace, assuring him, if he did so, that we were perfectly safe from capture. In half an hour we passed Pine Island, with the Champion, which did not appear to be straining herself, fully three miles astern. I was afterwards told that the captain of the Adieno held her back, fearing that if she crowded us again, we should run ashore, burst the boiler, or otherwise damage his steamer.

In an hour and a half after the passage of The Sisters Channel, we were off the bluff, within half a mile of the steamboat pier, which we saw crowded with people. It was plain that we had succeeded in creating an excitement, and not a few of us had some delicacy about landing in the presence of the multitude. The Champion still kept her relative distance from us, and was now more than a mile beyond Cleaver Island.

"Where shall we land?" I asked of Vallington through the tube, after Bob and I had considered the matter a little.

"Wherever you please, commodore," replied our chief.

"What do you say, Bob?" I added, turning to my companion.

"Can't we land at the boat pier, in front of the Institute?"

"No; there isn't water enough to float the Adieno. In fact the only safe place is the regular steamboat pier."

"I suppose my father is there, and I don't like to meet him just yet," replied Bob, earnestly.

"We can anchor within a few rods of the Institute pier, and land in the Splash," I suggested.

"I like that better."

"But the Splash would have to go three or four times to land the fellows, and the Champion would be upon us before we could all get ashore," I added.

I stated the plan and the objections to Vallington.

"Let us face the music like men," said he, decidedly.

"I think that is the better way," I continued to Bob. "So far as we have done wrong, let us acknowledge the corn, and take the consequences." ·

24*

Bob Hale assented, overcoming his modesty with an effort, and I headed the Adieno for the steamboat pier. I think we all felt a little bashful about landing in the presence of so many people. The students were directed to make no noisy demonstrations of any kind, and to repair directly to the school-room of the Institute, where Mr. Parasyte would soon find us, and where we hoped to make a final adjustment of all the difficulties.

As we approached the pier, the boat was "slowed down," and the fasts got ready for landing; and other work was done as regularly and properly as though we were all old steamboat men. At the regular time, I stopped her wheels, and she ran her bow up gently to the wharf, and the line was thrown ashore. A couple of turns of the wheels backward brought the Adieno to a stand-still, and our cruise was ended. Vallington let off steam, and we formed in a body, intending to march ashore as compactly as possible, in order to feel the full force of the bond of association.

With Vallington at the head of the procession, we landed. Some of the crowd hooted at us, others laughed, and a few steamboat owners berated us roundly. We heeded none of them, but made our way through the mob, up the pier. Before we reached the street, it suddenly occurred to me that I had left the Splash made fast to the stern of the steamer. I had forgotten her in the exciting whirl of events. When I told Bob Hale and Tom Rush that I must return for my boat, they volunteered to accompany me.

"Robert," said a stern voice, as we moved down the wharf.

We halted, and Bob's father confronted him.

"What does all this mean?" demanded Mr. Hale. "Are you one of those who ran away with the steamer?"

"I am, sir," replied Bob, squarely, but with due humility.

Mr. Hale bit his lips with chagrin. Probably he had hoped that his son was not one of the reckless fellows who had taken possession of the Adieno. But Bob was a noble fellow, and seldom gave his father any cause to complain of his conduct, — so seldom that he appeared to be appalled at the magnitude of the present offence.

"Robert was opposed to taking the steamer from

the first," I interposed, hoping to save him from some portion of his father's displeasure.

"I went with the rest of the fellows, and I am willing to bear my share of the blame."

"What does all this mean? What possessed you to do such a thing?" asked Mr. Hale.

"We could not endure the injustice of Mr. Parasyte any longer; that was the beginning of it. And when he came in the steamer to Pine Island, and took away our provisions, we ran off with the steamer rather than be starved out," answered Bob.

"What business had you on Pine Island?"

"We have been breaking away."

"Breaking away! I should think you had! Were you concerned in these disgraceful proceedings, Robert?"

"I was, sir. I am willing to own that I have done wrong."

Mr. Hale's stern look softened down, and I ventured to ask him to take a seat in my boat, and go over to the Institute, where he would have an opportunity to hear the whole story of the "breaking away," and judge for himself. During this conversation, a crowd had gathered around us, curious to know what had happened; and the charge we made against Mr. Parasyte was publicly proclaimed. Mr. Hale accepted my invitation, and we shoved off from the Adieno just as the Champion came up to the pier.

"Stop them! Stop them!" shouted the captain of the Adieno, as I was hoisting the jib.

No one ventured to stop a boat in which Mr. Hale, the most important person in the county, was seated.

"We want those boys!" called the angry captain again. "They are the ones who ran off with the boat."

"Captain Woelkers," said Mr. Hale, mildly.

"Ah, Mr. Hale!" exclaimed the captain, as he recognized the principal owner of the steamer he commanded.

"By whose authority did you take the Adieno to Pine Island to-day?"

"Mr. Parasyte wanted her, and I let him have her," stammered the captain.

"Did you consult the agent?"

"No, sir; he was not at home."

"Do you generally leave your boat with steam up without an engineer?"

"I never did before, but we needed every man to bring off the things on the island," replied Captain Woelkers, his confusion crimsoning his face.

" It appears that you have used the boat without authority, and permitted her to be taken from you by a parcel of boys. I will see you at my house this evening. You may fill away, Ernest, if you are ready."

Mr. Hale did not say another word, and I ran the Splash over to the Institute pier. I landed my passengers, and we all walked up to the school-room, where the rebels had by this time assembled.

" Henry Vallington, I am sorry to see you engaged in such a disgraceful affair as this," said Mr. Hale, when he met our leader.

" I am very glad you have come, sir, for I feel that we need counsel," replied Vallington. " Perhaps you will not consider the affair so disgraceful, after you have heard the whole truth."

" Nothing can justify your conduct in running away with the steamer. It is a miracle that you were not blown up, or sunk in the lake."

Vallington handed our distinguished guest one of the circulars he had procured at the printer's on his way up to the Institute, the " copy " of which had been given out before the " breaking away."

CHAPTER XXVI.

IN WHICH ERNEST FINDS A CHANGE IN THE MANAGEMENT OF THE INSTITUTE.

MR. HALE put on his spectacles and read the circular, which had been carefully prepared by several of the best scholars in the school; but he was already familiar with the facts it contained. He knew that Mr. Parasyte was a tyrant, and that he was very unpopular with the boys. It was a fact that only a few of the students remained at the Institute for any considerable length of time, and that its numbers had never equalled its capacity.

He had hardly finished reading the circular before Mr. Parasyte, followed by Poodles, Pearl, and the rest of the deserters, entered the hall. All of them had been passengers on the Champion, and of course they didn't feel very good after being beaten by the Adieno. Mr. Hale was evidently glad to see the principal of the academy, for he did not seem to know what to do after he had finished the circular.

"I am glad you have come, Mr. Parasyte," said he; "it seems these boys have been running away with one of our steamers."

"They have; and I hope you will punish the ring-leaders as they deserve," replied Mr. Parasyte, wiping his brow, as he was wont to do when excited.

"My son is one of them," added Mr. Hale, with a smile.

"Not one of the ringleaders, sir — by no means. Thornton, Rush, and Vallington are the leaders in this enterprise."

"No more than myself, father. I have done as much as they have, and I am willing to bear my share of the blame," said Bob.

The boys clapped their hands at this interposition. Bob was not a fellow to shirk when the time of settlement came.

"My boy behaves like a man, and I honor him for that," replied Mr. Hale, proudly; "but he shall be punished if the others are. Mr. Parasyte, things seem to be at rather loose ends in the Institute just now."

"Yes, sir; I am sorry to say they are. One bad boy can stir up a whirlwind of mischief," answered Mr. Parasyte, looking at me.

"These boys seem to be pretty well agreed in this matter."

"But this trouble has all been made by one boy —and that one is Ernest Thornton. I expelled him once; but out of regard for his uncle, to whom I am under great obligations, I reversed my sentence, and endeavored to reduce him to proper subjection."

"Have you seen this paper, Mr. Parasyte?" continued the visitor, handing him the circular. "It seems to be signed by nearly all the students in the Institute."

Mr. Parasyte took the printed document, and proceeded to read it. When he had gone far enough to comprehend the nature of the paper, he turned red; and when he came to the long array of signatures, he became very pale.

"May I inquire the object of this paper?" demanded the principal, with quivering lips.

"I'm sure I don't know. . I never saw or heard

of it till I entered this room," replied Mr. Hale. "I see that it is addressed to the parents of the students."

"I need not say that the statements contained in this circular are, without a single exception, infamous falsehoods and slanders. I think you know me well enough, Mr. Hale, to understand that justice and fairness have always characterized my dealings with my pupils."

Mr. Hale did not so understand it. He knew that the reverse of this statement was the truth. Mr. Parasyte then insisted on relating the facts connected with the "breaking away." He told the story of my misconduct, as he termed it, and embellished it with sundry flourishes about his own impartiality and magnanimity. He said that after it had been fairly proved that I had assaulted my schoolmate, in consideration of my previous good conduct, he had only required that I should apologize in private to the one I had injured. Forbearance could extend no farther than this; but I had even refused to make this slight reparation for the offence I had committed. Then I had openly disobeyed and insulted him in the presence of the whole school.

"Of course, after this," continued Mr. Parasyte, "I could do nothing more for him. My gentleness was not appreciated; my leniency was despised. My mistake was in treating him too kindly — in not resorting to the strong arm in the beginning. Then, as I might have expected of such an obdurate boy, I was subjected to a personal assault."

"But all the boys seemed to be on his side," said the matter-of-fact Mr. Hale.

"Very true. Thornton keeps a boat, and almost any boy may be bought or sold with a boat. He has sailed them on the lake, and won them by his arts."

"Isn't it possible that there was some mistake in the matter of the quarrel between Thornton and Poodles?"

"It is quite impossible that there should have been any mistake," replied Mr. Parasyte, with a look of injured innocence. "I investigated the matter very carefully and impartially."

"I should really like to hear what the boys have to say about it," added Mr. Hale.

"It would be useless for you to talk with them, and it would be an insult to me for you to do so. Do you doubt my word, Mr. Hale? Do you think I have not told you the truth?" said the principal, rather warmly.

"But there may be some mistake."

"I have said that it was quite impossible there should be any mistake."

"Have you any objections to my asking the boys a few questions, Mr. Parasyte?"

"Certainly I have. I am not willing to be arraigned and tried before my own school."

"O, very well!" exclaimed Mr. Hale, nodding his head significantly; and without saying anything more, he left the school-room.

The students felt that they had a friend in Mr. Hale, and even did not fear a prosecution for running away with the steamer. We judged that the captain of the Adieno would have to bear all the blame of that occurrence.

"What are these circulars for?" demanded Mr. Parasyte, when the visitor had departed. "Vallington, as the ringleader in this conspiracy, I call upon you for an answer."

"Those whose names are signed to the paper intend to send them to their parents."

"They do — do they?" exclaimed the principal, with compressed lips. "Are you aware that published slanders of this kind subject those who utter them to a severe penalty?"

"We can prove all we assert, and should be glad of an opportunity to do so," replied Vallington, firmly.

"There is not a word of truth in the paper," added Mr. Parasyte, wiping his brow.

He walked up and down the platform two or three times in silence. With him the case was desperate. He knew not what to do. He had learned that the students would not be browbeaten or bullied.

"Scholars," said he, at last, "I think we are all too much fatigued and excited to consider this difficult problem this afternoon. In spite of the ill treatment I have received at your hands, I am still your friend, as I have always been. By and by you will see that you have done wrong. To-morrow

25 *

morning, if you will meet at the usual hour in the school-room, I shall have a proposition to make, which I am confident will restore peace to the Parkville Liberal Institute. You are dismissed now, for the day."

Mr. Parasyte left the hall, and we held a meeting there on our own account. If the principal did not know what to do, we were no better off, and we finally separated without any fixed plans. We agreed to meet in the school-room in the morning, though we all doubted whether Mr. Parasyte would have any proposition to submit. The students decided not to send the circulars to their parents until the next day.

We wanted advice, and our hope was with Mr. Hale. At Vallington's suggestion, half a dozen of us were appointed a committee to wait upon him. He had expressed a desire to hear "the other side" of the case. We went to Mr. Hale's house, and found there Mr. Hardy, the assistant teacher, who had been discharged. We told our story, and related the facts as they occurred. Mr. Hardy said nothing in our presence, and we left him with Mr.

Hale, who, we afterwards learned, had sent for him.

Bob invited me to spend the night with him, and having no home now, I was glad to accept. After supper, I was called into the library, and questioned at great length by Mr. Hale and Mr. Hardy in regard to the affairs of the Institute. While we were thus engaged, Bob was sent to deliver several notes to prominent and wealthy men in the place. At seven o'clock there were not less than half a dozen of the "heavy men" of Parkville in the library.

Of course Bob and I did not know what was going on, but we were confident that the affairs of the Institute were under discussion. At a later hour, Mr. Hale and another gentleman drove off, in a buggy, towards the cottage of my uncle, where I heard one of them say they were going. Bob and I went to bed, tired out, and did not ascertain what had been done by the gentlemen who assembled that evening.

At nine o'clock in the forenoon of the next day, the students were all in their seats, in the school-room; but Mr. Parasyte did not appear. It was reported that there were half a dozen gentlemen with him in his office, and that my uncle Amos was one of them. I was astonished at this intelligence. I subsequently heard that he was there on business, and hardly spoke a word during a long and stormy interview between Mr. Parasyte and his visitors.

The clock on the school-house struck ten, and still Mr. Parasyte did not come. It was deeply impressed upon our minds that something was about to happen, and we waited with intense anxiety for the event. At half past eleven o'clock, Mr. Parasyte entered the school-room. He looked sad and subdued, and his coming was the signal for a breathless silence among the boys. It was evident that he had a proposition to make.

"Young gentlemen, I appear before you now for the last time," said he.

He paused, and his words made a tremendous sensation, though, I am happy to say, there was no demonstration of any kind. We looked upon him as a fallen man.

"I have sold the Parkville Liberal Institute to a company composed of the citizens of this town, who have made me an offer for the property, so liberal that I could not afford to refuse it. Until about a week ago, my relations with the students have been exceedingly pleasant. I shall not allude to recent events. I take my leave with many regrets, and I sincerely desire that prosperity and happiness may attend you in the future. Good by."

"Good by," replied a large number of the boys, and Mr. Parasyte bowed and left the room.

As he went out at one door, the "company" entered at another. Mr. Hale went upon the platform, and repeated what Mr. Parasyte had told us, that the Institute had been purchased by a number of the citizens of Parkville, and in future its affairs would be managed by a board of trustees, of which he had the honor to be chairman. The trustees had just appointed Mr. Hardy as principal,—here he was interrupted by a spontaneous burst of cheers, —and the school would be reorganized by him in the afternoon. The "boarders" were requested to write to their parents and guardians, informing them of the change.

Mr. Hale dismissed the students, after he had assured them that the domestic part of the establishment would remain as before. The boys went out upon the play ground, and gave three rousing cheers for the new company, trustees, and principal. I went home to dinner with Bob, and learned that the purchase of the Institute had been contemplated for some months, by prominent citizens, who were aware that the school was badly managed. They acted, many of them, simply as business men, for the interests of the town. The Institute was "running down," and they had taken this step to build it up. They knew that Mr. Hardy was a true man and a good teacher, and as he was popular among the boys, he was promptly elected principal.

Mr. Hale told Bob and me that the conduct of the students in "breaking away" was strongly condemned by the gentlemen who had discussed the affair, and he by no means approved of it himself; but the injustice of Mr. Parasyte had provoked them to such a degree that the misdemeanor was palliated, if not excused, and it was deemed best to say nothing about it. The mortgage which my uncle held was paid, and he had fled the instant the business was finished.

Mr. Parasyte had long and obstinately refused to sell the property, even for a third more than its actual value; but finally, convinced that the Institute would not succeed under his administration, he had yielded the point. The next day he left Parkville, with his family, "bag and baggage;" and so disagreeable was he to me, that I hoped I never should see his face again.

In the afternoon we went to school, and Mr. Hardy appeared upon the platform. We attempted to cheer him, but he silenced us. He made quite a speech, in which, however, he did not allude to recent events, and in half an hour the students were all at work on the old track. While I was in school that afternoon for the last time, as I believed, I received a note from my uncle. It was as brief as his speech. "If you wish to return to your home, you may." This, with the signature, was all it contained. I went home that night, but my uncle did not see me — would not see me.

I went to school as usual for several months, until

the following spring, when an event occurred which made me a wanderer on the earth; which sent me to "SEEK AND FIND" the mother, for whom I longed and prayed in my loneliness, and which shall be related in another story.

Our rebellion at the Institute had been successful. We had driven the tyrant from his throne, and seated another person in his place, who was fit to teach and to rule. Mr. Hardy was, perhaps, more severe than his predecessor, but he was just and fair. He had no favorites — at least none who did not win their high place in his esteem by being faithful and earnest in all things. Certainly he never gave the students occasion even to think of such a doubtful expedient as "BREAKING AWAY."